INTO THE CLA

RELIGIOUS EDUCATION IN THE LEAVING CERTIFICATE

World Religions

Philip Barnes

Series Editors
Eoin G. Cassidy and Patrick M. Devitt

VERITAS

First published 2003 by
Veritas Publications
7/8 Lower Abbey Street
Dublin 1
Ireland
Email publications@veritas.ie
Website www.veritas.ie

ISBN 1 85390 701 4

10 9 8 7 6 5 4 3 2 1

A catalogue record for this book is available from the British Library.

Cover design by Bill Bolger
Printed in the Republic of Ireland by Betaprint Ltd, Dublin

Veritas books are printed on paper made from the wood pulp of managed forests. For every tree felled, at least one tree is planted, thereby renewing natural resources.

Contents

Introduction

September 2003 saw the introduction of the Leaving Certificate Religious Education Syllabus by the Department of Education and Science. For those concerned to promote a religious sensibility in young Irish adults it is hard to exaggerate the importance of this event. It both represents a formal recognition by society of the value of religious education in the academic lives of second-level students, and it also reflects the importance which Irish society attaches to promoting the personal growth of students, including their spiritual and moral development. Religious education offers young people the opportunity to understand and interpret their experience in the light of a religious world-view. Furthermore, in and through an engagement with the RE Syllabus at Leaving Certificate level, students will learn a language that will enable them both to articulate their own faith experience and to dialogue with those of different faiths or non-theistic stances.

The Department of Education Syllabus is to be welcomed in that it gives recognition to the role that religious education plays in the human development of the young person. It is not an exaggeration to say that religious education is the capstone of the school's educational response to the young person's search for meaning and values. In this context, it encourages students to reflect upon their awareness of themselves as unique individuals with roots in a community network of family, friends and parish. Furthermore, it allows students to acknowledge and reflect upon their relationship to a God who cares for them and for the world in which we live. Finally, it gives students access to the universal nature of the quest for truth, beauty and goodness. Most of these themes are addressed sympathetically in the section entitled *The Search for Meaning and Values*. In particular, this section is to be welcomed because it offers the possibility for students to grapple with theistic and non-theistic world-views in a context that is hospitable to religious belief.

A critical dimension of the young person's educational journey is the growth in understanding of their own culture and the manner in which culture shapes their outlook on the world. The Religious Education Syllabus not only addresses the manner in which religion (and in particular Christianity) has shaped Irish culture over many centuries, but it also provides an extremely valuable platform from which to critique aspects of the relationship between faith and culture in the contemporary world. The section entitled *Religion: The Irish Experience* addresses the former concern by showing pupils the manner in which the Christian religion has contributed to the belief patterns and values of Irish society. It also alerts them to the depths of religious belief that predate by many centuries, even millennia, the arrival of Christianity in Ireland; and it also connects them to the cultural richness that links Ireland to the European continent. In this context, the devotional revolution that took place in Ireland (including the extraordinary growth in religious orders from 1850-1930) is a topic that could be expanded. The missionary outreach of the Catholic Church in Ireland in the last hundred years is worthy of special mention. Finally, students studying this section should be encouraged to acknowledge the ambiguities that have attended the presence of religion in Ireland over the centuries; to see on the one hand the image of an island of saints and scholars, and on the other hand to note how 'lilies that fester smell far worse than weeds'.

In examining the manner in which faith and culture interact, the sections entitled *Religion and Science* and *Religion and Gender* make a valuable contribution to the Syllabus. These sections address topical issues that were controversial in the past and continue to be problematical even today. In treating of these two topics it is obviously important to avoid stereotypes – the acceptance of unexamined assumptions that mask or over-simply the truth to such an extent as to do a disservice to the seriousness of the issues involved. Likewise, the section on *World Religions* should be taught in a manner that is sensitive to the dangers of cultural and religious stereotypes. This section not only gives students a valuable introduction to the main religions in the world, but it also provides a cultural context for an awareness of the fact that the phenomenon of religion and the experience of religious belief is something that shapes people's understanding of themselves and their lifestyles across all cultural boundaries. Furthermore, it should never be forgotten that if, as Christians believe, God's Spirit is present in and through these religions, there is a need to study these religions precisely in order to discover aspects of God's presence in the world that has the capability to continually surprise.

In the Irish cultural context, Catholicism shapes the religious sensibilities and practices of the majority of young people. The Syllabus offers a generous acknowledgement of the importance of Christianity in the Irish context by providing two sections that focus on core aspects of the Christian faith. These are: *Christianity: origins and contemporary expressions* and *The Bible: Literature and Sacred text*. In this context, the Syllabus section on the Bible is to be welcomed. However, greater attention could be given to the role and significance of the Prophets in the Old Testament and to Paul in the New Testament. Furthermore, in studying the Bible it should never be forgotten that the primary reality is not the 'book' but rather the person of Christ and the community tradition grappling with this reality that is revealed in and through the Bible.

What is often in danger of being forgotten in an academic context is the importance of the fostering of attitudes and practices that promote personal growth. Religious education cannot be focused only on knowledge and understanding, because religion is primarily a way of celebrating life and, in particular, the spiritual dimension of life in and through the practices of worship, ritual and prayer. The Syllabus's recognition of this critical dimension of religious education through the section entitled *Worship, Ritual and Prayer* is to be welcomed. In addressing this section of the Syllabus it would be important to alert students to the great variety of spiritualities, prayer forms, mysticisms, rituals and styles of music that are to be found within the Christian tradition in order that students may have the possibility of exploring the richness of the spiritual dimension of their own tradition.

A key remit of the educational process is the fostering of moral maturity through a syllabus that allows students to engage in moral education. Not only is religious education particularly suited to facilitating this educational imperative, but the ethical character of human life is a core feature of all religions. The importance of this dimension of religious education is recognised in the provision of two sections entitled *Moral Decision Making* and *Issues of Justice and Peace*. There is nothing optional about the challenge to promote justice and peace. However, it is a topic that can all too easily be ideologically driven. Therefore, there is a special responsibility on those teaching this section to ensure that the instances of injustice cited, and the causes of injustice proposed, are grounded in solid research.

The challenges to Catholic religion teachers

Though religious education has been an integral part of Irish second-level schools long before the foundation of the state, it has not until now been possible to assess this work under the State examination system. The reason for this anomaly is the Intermediate Education Act (1878) which allowed for the teaching but forbade the State examination of religious education. The removal of this legal constraint on State examination of RE has provided the impetus for the introduction of the Junior Certificate Syllabus in September 2000 and the introduction of the Leaving Certificate Syllabus in September 2003. These changes are to be welcomed but they provide a number of major challenges to Catholic religion teachers that should not be minimised.

In the *first* place, Catholic religion teachers have to attend to the danger that the new Syllabus will lead to a weakening of a commitment to catechesis in second level schools. The catechetical project of faith formation is built around six key pillars: knowledge of the faith; liturgical/sacramental education; moral formation; learning to pray; education for community life, including a fostering of the ecumenical character of Christian community, and finally, missionary initiative and inter-religious dialogue. Clearly, the RE Leaving Certificate Syllabus does give attention to many of the above themes, including the key catechetical concerns of attitude or value formation and the development of commitments. However, the emphasis in the Syllabus is undoubtedly upon the acquiring of knowledge, understanding and knowledge-based skills, all of which undoubtedly place it under the rubric of religious education rather than catechesis. The religion teacher ought to value the distinctive approaches to religion reflected in both catechesis and religious education. Both are important because both contribute in distinctive ways to the religious development of the young person. Catechesis aims at maturity of faith whereas religious education aims at knowledge and understanding of the faith.

From the point of view of the religion teacher, the teaching can have a different tone at different times. On one occasion, it might have a 'showing how' or catechetical tone, one that assumes a shared faith experience and encourages active participation. At another time it can have an educational or 'explaining' tone that invites pupils to stand back from religion to a certain extent, so that they can gain a more objective understanding of what is being taught. The Religious Education Syllabus should be taught in a manner that keeps both of these approaches in balance. In a similar vein, the presence of RE on the Leaving Certificate curriculum should not distract teachers from acknowledging that the religious development of young people happens in many contexts, which are distinct, though complementary. It can take place at home, in the parish, with friends as well as in school. Furthermore, even in the school it can take place at a whole series of levels including liturgy, prayer and projects that encourage an awareness of the need to care for those in most need.

In the *second* place, teachers have to attend to the scope and range of the aims of the Syllabus, one that seeks both to introduce students to a broad range of religious traditions and to the non-religious interpretation of life as well as providing students with the opportunity to develop an informed and critical understanding of the Christian tradition. In this context, teachers have to balance the need to promote tolerance for and mutual understanding of those of other or no religious traditions, alongside the need to give explicit attention to the Christian faith claims that Jesus is the Son of God and that he died to save us and to unite us with God and one another. Similarly, in teaching Christianity, teachers need to give attention to the role and significance of the Church from a Catholic perspective. It should never be forgotten that the idea of the Church as 'people of God', 'body of Christ' and 'temple of the Holy Spirit' is one that is at the heart of Catholic self-understanding.

In a similar vein, the Syllabus encourages students to engage critically with a wide variety of ethical codes with a view to the development of a moral maturity. Teachers will have to balance this approach with the way in which morality is viewed within the Christian tradition under the heading of discipleship – Jesus invites people to follow *him* rather than an ethical code or vision. Furthermore, from a Christian perspective, morality is never simply or even primarily concerned with a listing of moral prohibitions, rather it situates the ethical dimension of human nature within the context of a belief in a forgiving God. Finally, it should not be forgotten that it does not make sense to teach morality in too abstract a manner. Morality is something preeminently practical and at all times needs to be brought down to the level of real people – those who struggle with the demands of conscience in their lives. From a Catholic perspective, one has in the lives of the saints a multitude of examples of the manner in which people have attempted to follow the call to discipleship that is Christian morality.

Finally, nobody concerned with the seriousness of the challenge facing schools to promote moral maturity could be unaware of the importance of the contemporary challenge posed to the promotion of societal and religious values by the rise of a relativist and/or subjectivist ethos. In this context, the teaching of the broad variety of moral codes will have to be done in a manner that draws students' attention to the importance of acknowledging the objective nature of morality as opposed to accepting uncritically either a relativist or a subjectivist standpoint. In the light of the need to critique an exaggerated acceptance of pluralism, there is also a need to acknowledge that not all theories are equally valid, and moral decision-making is not simply a matter of applying one's own personal preference.

What is proposed in these commentaries
Given the breadth and scope of the Syllabus it is undoubtedly true that teachers will have to attend to the wide variety of sections in the Syllabus which demand a breadth of knowledge that some may find a little daunting. Even though it is not envisaged that teachers would attempt to teach all ten sections

of the Syllabus to any one group of students, nevertheless, the Syllabus will make demands upon teachers that can only be met if there are support services in place. For example, apart from the need to ensure the publishing of good quality teaching and learning resources, the schools themselves will need to ensure that appropriate resources – books, CDs, internet and videos – are provided. Finally, teachers will need to be provided with appropriate in-service training. It is to furthering this goal of providing good quality teaching and learning resources that the present series of volumes is addressed.

The eleven volumes in this series of commentaries comprise an introductory volume (already published, *Willingly To School*) that reflects upon the challenge of RE as an examination subject, along with ten other volumes that mirror the ten sections in the Syllabus. These commentaries on the Syllabus have been published to address the critical issue of the need to provide resources for the teaching of the Syllabus that are both academically rigorous and yet accessible to the educated general reader. Although primarily addressed to both specialist and general teachers of religion and third-level students studying to be religion teachers, the commentaries will be accessible to parents of Leaving Certificate pupils and, in addition, it is to be hoped that they will provide an important focus for adults in parish-based or other religious education or theology programmes. In the light of this focus, each of the volumes is structured in order to closely reflect the content of the Syllabus and its order of presentation. Furthermore, they are written in clear, easily accessible language and each includes an explanation of new theological and philosophical perspectives.

The volumes offered in this series are as follows

Patrick M. Devitt:	*Willingly to School: Religious Education as an Examination Subject*
Eoin G. Cassidy:	*The Search for Meaning and Values*
Thomas Norris and Brendan Leahy:	*Christianity: Origins and Contemporary Expressions*
Philip Barnes:	*World Religions*
Patrick Hannon:	*Moral Decision Making*
Sandra Cullen:	*Religion and Gender*
John Murray:	*Issues of Justice and Peace*
Christopher O'Donnell:	*Worship, Prayer and Ritual*
Benedict Hegarty:	*The Bible: Literature and Sacred Text*
John Walsh:	*Religion: The Irish Experience*
Fachtna McCarthy and Joseph McCann:	*Religion and Science*

Thanks are due to the generosity of our contributors who so readily agreed to write a commentary on each of the sections in the new Leaving Certificate Syllabus. Each of them brings to their commentary both academic expertise and a wealth of experience in the teaching of their particular area. In the light of this, one should not underestimate the contribution that they will make to the work of preparing teachers for this challenging project. Thanks are also due to our publishers, Veritas. Their unfailing encouragement and practical support has been of inestimable value to us and has ensured that these volumes saw the light of day. Finally, we hope that you the reader will find each of these commentaries helpful as you negotiate the paths of a new and challenging syllabus.

Eoin G. Cassidy
Patrick M. Devitt
Series Editors

Preface

The purpose of this book is to provide a commentary on the *World Religions* option of the new Leaving Certificate Religious Education Syllabus. The content of the syllabus has determined the content of this study. Likewise the order and structure of presentation follow that of the syllabus. In other words, it is a book for which I claim no originality. My task was to put intellectual flesh on the bare bones supplied by others. At one point only have I introduced a section that does not correspond to the syllabus: in each of the chapters dealing with a major world religion I have provided a brief overview of the religion's history, beliefs and internal divisions. I felt that such a context was needed for the remainder of the required content to be fully appreciated and understood. It may also be pertinent to note that in some places the issues that I identify and discuss are of my own choosing, in that the syllabus allows for individual choice and interest. For example, the syllabus requires a description of three religious trends in contemporary Ireland, but it does not specify the material to be covered. Naturally there is scope for difference of opinion at this point. Others may legitimately fulfil the requirements of the syllabus by identifying and studying different trends from those I discuss. Naturally too my interpretation of things comes across in much of what I write. There is no requirement on anyone to agree with my interpretation. I offer mine as a stimulus to further thinking. The individual spirit in which I write leads me to encourage the development of individuality in others.

A wide range of religious topics is covered in the syllabus, some of which one might not have anticipated in a study of this kind. The breadth of the syllabus and its diversity mean that there is certain superficiality about much of what I say. I have not been able to indulge myself and write at length with suitable qualification. Moreover, greater latitude of purpose might have permitted the discussion of a number of issues that have come to the fore in recent scholarly studies of religion. For example, I am aware that the presentation of the different religions follows a traditional Western pattern that tends to impose a degree of religious orthodoxy and uniformity upon them that is not always evident in experience. The notion of popular religion and the extent to which the different religions have accommodated themselves to local situations and local indigenous cultures are also overlooked. One cannot attend to everything. My hopes will be fulfilled if I succeed in inspiring some of my readers to turn from this introductory study to some of the more substantial textbooks in the field of religious studies.

I would like to thank Fr Patrick Devitt and Fr Eoin Cassidy for the invitation to contribute to the series of which this book is one contribution. I found them to be undemanding and generous editors. Finally, I would like to thank my wife Sandra for undertaking more than her fair share of domestic duties over the last number of months while I have been more consistently engaged in writing than usual. Promises of undivided attention in the future may not convince, but at least commitment endures.

I

The Phenomenon of Religion

1.1   RELIGION AS A WORLD-WIDE PHENOMENON

There is a rich variety of beliefs, activities and customs commonly designated as religious: apologising to God for one's sinfulness, bowing before an image of the Buddha, scattering ashes on the River Ganges, beating one's chest in memory of the violent death of Hussein, a member of the prophet Muhammad's family, tea-ceremonies in Japan, consulting a shaman, and so on. The diversity of religion naturally raises the question of definition. To what does the word 'religion' apply? We speak of Buddhism, Christianity and Hinduism as religions, but is there any belief or practice common to them? The Christian notion of a single, almighty, all-powerful God does not fit the cultural and religious reality of Hinduism particularly well, and in the case of Theravada Buddhism, does not fit at all: God and the gods are superfluous to the pursuit of salvation. What about a more nebulous concept of deity, say the existence of a spiritual being (or spiritual beings): does this provide a minimum content by which religious activities and beliefs can be distinguished from non-religious activities and beliefs? Certainly most religions affirm the existence of a spiritual being, but do all? Again Theravada Buddhism has been quoted as an exception by a number of authorities. Such difficulties have suggested to some scholars that the problem of definition is intractable and that the cause of understanding religion would be better served by simply getting on with the task of describing and explaining religious phenomena. Such a position has been pursued by the eminent, British philosopher and phenomenologist of religion, Ninian Smart (who died in 2001). Rather than attempt to construct a definition of religion, which, he believes, experience shows will be inadequate in some respect, he advocates that we look at the different religions (following common usage) and analyse their nature. In his view, a religion reveals itself to be composed of a number of different dimensions. These are:

- the practical and ritual dimension
- the experiential and emotional dimension
- the narrative or mythic dimension
- the doctrinal and philosophical dimension
- the ethical and legal dimension
- the social and institutional dimension
- the material dimension (by which is meant buildings, works of art, and sacred places)

Although Smart contended that these dimensions are present in all the different religions he acknowledged that different religions place varying emphasis on them. For example, Buddhism stresses the experiential dimension of religion, and attaches much less importance to the narrative or mythic dimension; Protestant Christianity emphasises the doctrinal and philosophical dimension, and so on. It would be an interesting exercise to apply Smart's dimensional analysis of religion to the different religions and religious movements that we will be considering in subsequent chapters.

Types of religion

There are different ways of categorising religion. One popular categorisation is to distinguish between prophetic and mystical religions: Christianity, Islam and Judaism belong to the former category, whereas Buddhism, Hinduism and Sikhism belong to the latter category. Prophets are spokespersons (historically, typically *spokesmen*) for God. They receive a message from God, which they then pass on to others. Focus falls on the revealed 'word of God'. Given the divine origin of the message it is invariably remembered and transmitted in written form, hence the production of Sacred Scriptures such as the Hebrew and Christian Bibles and the Qur'an. The proper response to the message of God is obedience. Mystics, by contrast, experience union with the divine. The religious focus falls on the need for adherents to 'authenticate' the experience for themselves in their own lives. Even though mystics produce religious texts and writings it is made clear by them that the texts are useful only to the extent that they serve to direct others to seek immediate experience for themselves. Prophets typically accentuate the transcendence and otherness of God. God is 'high and lifted up'; his mystery is only penetrated when he chooses to reveal himself. Prophetic religions speak of the 'grace of God': God is experienced only when he chooses to reveal himself. Mystical religion tends to accentuate the closeness of God. In some traditions, Advaita Vedanta Hinduism, for example, there is the notion that God and the disciple become one: the individual participates and lives in God. Meditation replaces worship and salvation is achieved by commitment to the mystical path and by self-effort. Is this characterisation of two types of religion convincing? It does carry force, but only up to a point. There are difficulties, in that there are prophetic elements within Hinduism that exalt the transcendence of God and there are mystical elements within the theistic, prophetic religions that exalt the closeness of God. Christianity is a good example, with some writers tracing the Christian mystical tradition back to the New Testament. Christians are implored by John the Apostle to 'abide in Christ' and St Paul speaks of the Spirit of God indwelling believers. In response to such observations, Ninian Smart has maintained that rather than divide religions into prophetic and mystical categories we should instead view each religion as a combination of both prophetic and mystical elements. In Islam, the prophetic element predominates over the mystical, though it does not exclude it altogether. In Hinduism, by contrast, the mystical element predominates. In Christianity, according to Smart, the balance between prophetic and mystical is about equal: one element does not predominate over the other.

The categorising of religions into prophetic and mystical categories is only one of a number of different ways of distinguishing religions. One straightforward way to categorise the different religions is to trace their ancestry. On this understanding Islam and Judaism trace their roots back to Judaism. Christianity emerged historically out of Judaism, and Islam emerged historically out of Christianity and Judaism. Similarly Buddhism emerged out of the Buddha's rejection of certain elements of Hinduism, like the notion of caste, though he did affirm other elements, rebirth for example. Another way of categorising religions is in terms of their concept of deity. We can distinguish between polytheistic, pantheistic and monotheistic religious traditions. In polytheistic religions, such as Primal Religion (on one interpretation), popular Hinduism and Shamanism, the existence of many gods is affirmed. Pantheistic traditions, such as Mahayana Buddhism and certain schools of Hinduism, identify the divine as present in all things. Monotheistic religion, as illustrated by Christianity, Islam and Judaism, maintain that there is only one true God, the infinite and personal Creator, whose perfect character is love, holiness, righteousness, justice, mercy, kindness and compassion. This one God rules over all. A variation on this theme is to trace the evolutionary history of religion (or at least what is supposed to be the evolutionary history of religion) from animism to polytheism to pantheism and then to monotheism. We will look at this theory more closely when we consider Primal Religion later in this chapter.

Global distribution of religion

In most countries of the world, a majority of people (over 50 per cent) are adherents of the same religion. In most nations where Christians make up the majority, the majority of the population are adherents of a single religious body (such as the Greek Orthodox Church in Greece, the Catholic Church in Poland, or the Evangelical Lutheran Church in Norway). Either Christianity or Islam is the predominant religion in most places. Even though a larger number of nations are predominantly Christian, it is sometimes claimed that the influence of Christianity is not as great as that of Islam on its adherents. In other words, Muslims are more likely to be religiously committed than Christians.

Christianity is the world's largest religion, with perhaps as many as two billion adherents; it can claim to have a significant number of followers on every continent. Eastern and Western Europe, the countries of North and South America are all predominantly Christian – at least in a formal sense. Much of Africa, particularly Central and Southern Africa is Christian, as are Australia and New Zealand.

We have already spoken of religious commitment and introduced the notion of *formal* membership of a religion. Religious commitment typically denotes participation in religious activities, whereas formal membership may simply mean that an individual chooses to describe himself or herself as belonging to a religion or is regarded by some religion as an adherent, perhaps on the basis of having undergone a rite of passage as an infant or child. The important point to note is that formal membership need not denote any real religious commitment in terms of practice or public expression of religion. Formal membership without any real commitment is often referred to as nominal membership. The statistics to which we refer provide information on the formal membership of religions only; they provide little insight into the nature and commitment of those identified as formally religious.

Islam has about one billion three hundred thousand adherents. Ninety per cent of Muslims belong to Sunni Islam and 10 per cent belong to Shi'a Islam (this distinction is explained in Chapter 4). Most countries throughout the Middle East are Muslim, countries such as Egypt, Iran, Iraq, Jordan and Syria. A large number of countries in Africa, particularly North Africa, are also Muslim: Algeria, Libya, Morocco, Tunisia, Somalia and Sudan. In the East, Islam is the dominant religion in Bangladesh, Pakistan and Indonesia.

Hinduism, the world's third largest religion, makes up the majority of the population in three nations: India, Nepal and Mauritius. The majority of the world's Hindus live in India, though the nation as a whole is only about 80 per cent Hindu, and is officially a secular state. Altogether there are about nine hundred million Hindus. In Nepal a higher proportion of the population are Hindus than in India. Nepal is the world's only official Hindu state. Freedom of worship is protected, but the official state religion is Hinduism. In Mauritius, a majority of 54 per cent of the population is Hindu.

The world's fourth largest organised religion, Buddhism, is the religion of the majority of the population in about ten countries in Asia, particularly South-East Asia, countries such as Cambodia, Laos, Thailand, and Vietnam. Buddhism is also very important historically and culturally in several other Asian countries, but is no longer cited as the main religion by at least 50 per cent of the population. In China and North Korea, Buddhism was forcibly suppressed by Communist regimes. In South Korea Christianity has recently made sufficient gains to displace Buddhism as the religion of the majority of the population. Currently, many people in traditional Buddhist countries such as Korea and China are embracing Christianity, while Buddhism in turn is gaining increasing numbers of converts among Westerners in places such as Europe, Australia, and the United States. There are about three hundred and sixty million Buddhists worldwide.

Sikhism does not make up the majority of the population in

any nation. Sikhism does, however, make up the majority of the population in the Indian Province of the Punjab. Sikhism is often called the world's fifth largest organised religion, and with nearly twenty million adherents, it is larger than Judaism. For many Sikhs not having a state of their own is an issue of great importance and the Punjabi independence movement is hotly debated in the region and in the Sikh community worldwide. Some Sikhs feel that an emphasis on achieving their own independent political state is overly divisive and draws undue attention away from the profound theological and spiritual message of their religion.

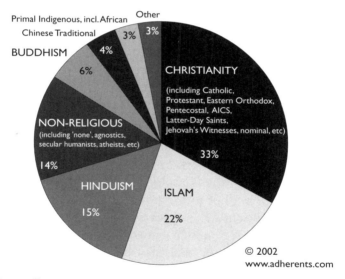

Religious adherents as a percentage of the world's population

Jews make up the majority (83 per cent) of the population in the country of Israel. Interestingly, a large number of Israel's Jews are secular, i.e. non-observant or agnostic or atheist. Religious Jews are in the minority in Israel. A larger number of Jews live in the United States than in Israel, and a higher proportion of American Jews are religious (i.e., practise Judaism or profess some form of belief in Judaism). There are about fourteen million Jews world-wide.

The religion of Europe

In the late Middle Ages, Roman Catholicism dominated religious life within Europe. The Pope enjoyed unchallenged religious supremacy. The Church enjoyed the support of Emperor and people. Since then, as a result of reformation and secularisation, the influence of Christianity has declined, and if we equate the Christian Churches with religion, then we might be tempted to conclude that religion has declined. But to rush to such a conclusion may be both premature and controversial.

In a typical European country there is one large Church, superior in numbers, which until the twentieth century was closely tied to the state, or which may still be closely tied to the state. Generally, the Catholic Church is predominant in southern Europe, while Protestant national Churches are predominant in northern Europe (Ireland being an exception). Germany takes an intermediate position, and is also an exception to the rule: here the Catholic and the Protestant Churches are almost equally strong. In southern Europe, in traditionally Catholic countries like Spain and Italy, the Catholic Church still has an important social position, but not to the extent it had some decades ago. Secularisation has had its impact on these countries; it also had its effect on the relationship between state and Church. The concordats, for example, that had been signed by the fascist regimes of Italy and Spain and the Vatican have been partially revised. If we look at the northern European counterpart, the five Scandinavian countries, we see Protestant national state Churches. The social relevance of these Churches has greatly decreased – even more than the Catholic Church in southern Europe – but state / Church structures still exist; only Sweden has abolished its state Church (in the year 2000).

The broad division between Catholic Southern Europe and Protestant Northern Europe also correlates to a distinctive pattern of religious participation. The populations of Southern Europe record higher levels of church attendance than the populations of Northern Europe. But it is equally true that across Europe, perhaps with the exception of Catholic Ireland, fewer people are attending church regularly than thirty or forty years ago. This is particularly apparent in such countries as England and Wales. The story of institutional decline, however, does not reveal the full story of the nature of religious change within European society. Despite falling levels of religious participation, there is also strong evidence that the population of Europe is still relatively religious in terms of belief. On average 70 per cent of Europeans believe in God, and interestingly, there is no significant difference between Southern Europe and Northern Europe. Traditional Catholic countries may have higher levels of religious participation, but this does not translate into higher levels of religious belief.

England and Wales are highly secularised countries, with low levels of church attendance. The majority of the population, however, describes itself as Christian and most people mark 'rites of passage' such as birth, marriage and death with Christian ceremonies. Self-designation, however, may disguise the true nature of religious decline, for although people may describe themselves as Christian, the evidence shows that only a small proportion of the population actually attends Christian worship on a typical Sunday. This phenomenon broadly holds across Europe, and it has been described by one sociologist as 'believing without belonging'.

Ireland is one of the most religious countries in Europe. Whereas the average church attendance on a typical Sunday is 29 per cent across Europe, in Ireland a figure of 59 per cent is recorded. Interestingly, the figure for Northern Ireland is 49 per cent, considerably lower, but actually the second highest level of church attendance in Europe. Does this mean that both countries are unaffected by the process of secularisation? We address this question a little later in this chapter in the section entitled 'Religious Trends in Ireland'.

Although the story of institutional religious decline across Europe may not be true everywhere, it is generally true. By contrast, Charismatic fellowships and house-churches have grown considerably over the last forty years or so, and of course immigration into Europe over the last fifty years has also increased the numbers of those who adhere to religions other than Christianity. In Britain and Germany, for example, there are now quite large Muslim communities. Mosques, temples and gurdwaras exist alongside churches in most large European cities. Equally there has been a growth of new religions and 'unorthodox' religious movements across Europe. Religious choice has never been greater, even though the majority remain within the religion of their birth and upbringing. There are commentators, Rodney Stark for example, who claim that increasing competition between religions has the effect of raising the levels of religious participation across society. Consequently as new religions and movements begin to make their presence felt in Europe so we can anticipate religious growth. This may still mean that the traditional Christian Churches will continue to decline, but overall the participation in religion will increase as individuals take advantage of new opportunities to join emerging religious groups.

Religious traditions in Ireland

The predominant religious tradition in Ireland is Christianity. Both the Anglican Church of Ireland and the Roman Catholic Church trace their origins to the ministry of St Patrick and the founding of the Celtic Church in Ireland, some time in the fifth century. Monasticism thrived in the sixth and seventh centuries and played a hugely significant role in the life of the Irish Church, and through the work of missionaries from Ireland, in the life of the Church across Europe. In time Celtic Christianity and Roman Catholic Christianity became one. It is a moot point to enquire when they became one, or whether they were always spiritually, if not institutionally one. In any case the religion of the Irish throughout the Middle Ages was exclusively Catholic, if not in the sense that Catholicism was able to banish local beliefs and customs, which were held and practised alongside and even integrated into Christianity, at least exclusive in the sense that all formally professed Christianity. The Reformation in Europe in the sixteenth century eventually made its presence felt in Ireland, when James I (1603–25) in an attempt to 'consolidate' his rule in Ireland planted English Anglican and Scottish Presbyterian 'settlers' in six of the counties of Ulster – in 1542 Henry VIII had declared that he and his heirs would be 'Kings of Ireland'. In the succeeding centuries of British rule religious and political differences were accentuated by legitimate Catholic grievances over land and discriminatory practices. British rule in Ireland was interpreted by most Irish, if not most Protestants (who were a significant minority in the country), as a period of English domination and even occupation. Ireland was partitioned in 1921, into Northern Ireland and the Republic of Ireland, a partition symbolic in some respects of a deeper partition in the 'Irish' mind over religion.

All the main Christian Churches treat the island of Ireland in its entirety as one unit for purposes of organisation. Currently, about 75 per cent of the population of Ireland as a whole profess to be Roman Catholic, with the Church of Ireland and Presbyterian each commanding the allegiance of about 6-7 per cent of the total population. Such statistics no doubt present a somewhat inflated impression of the significance of religion, but in reality they tell us little about the nature and depth of religious commitment: many are churchgoers, others are nominal Christians and do not practise on a regular basis, still others are Christian in name only.

Catholics make up 91.6 per cent of the population of the Republic and about 40 per cent of the population of Northern

Ireland. The leader of the Church in Ireland is the Archbishop of Armagh, the Primate of All-Ireland, and is usually a cardinal. The Church has twenty-six dioceses and four provinces each under a metropolitan archbishop. There are over 1,300 parishes, about 3,400 diocesan or secular priests and some 20,000 members of religious orders in Ireland. The Irish Church has a strong missionary outreach with nearly three thousand priests, brothers and nuns active in more than ninety countries across the globe.

The Church of Ireland is a self-governing Church within Anglicanism and is therefore in communion with the See of Canterbury. Although it retained episcopacy, its beliefs and practices are ordered by an appeal to the Bible. The leader of the Church of Ireland is the Archbishop of Armagh. His is a 'primacy of honour' and not a 'primacy of authority'. The Church has twelve dioceses, approximately 470 parishes and some 540 ministers (who can be male or female). Up until 1869 the Church of Ireland was the state Church in Ireland and since then its chief legislative body has been the General Synod made up of the bishops and representatives of clergy and laity. In the Republic just over 2 per cent of the population profess to be members of the Church of Ireland, while the percentage in Northern Ireland is about 18 per cent: Church membership is declining in both jurisdictions.

The Presbyterian Church in Ireland is strongly represented in Northern Ireland, claiming the allegiance of over 21 per cent of the population; in the South less than 0.4 per cent profess allegiance. The Presbyterian Church follows a broadly democratic system of Church government, expressed through elected elders and ministers of the local congregation, presbyteries (of which there are twenty-one in Ireland), synods with wider representation, and finally the general assembly of ministers and elders elected by the presbyteries throughout Ireland. The leader of the Presbyterian Church is the moderator, always a minister, who is elected for a one-year term of office. The ministry was opened to women in 1972, though not without considerable opposition from more conservative elements in the Church. The Bible, as with all Protestant Churches and denominations, is the final court of appeal in Presbyterianism. Christian belief and practice should be regulated by the teachings of the Bible and the example and practice of the early Church as described in the Bible. The Westminster Confession of Faith, drafted by the Puritan 'divines' at Westminster in 1643, is regarded as a *subordinate* standard, in the sense that its theological content is believed to systematise and summarise the teaching of the Bible.

About 9 per cent of the population of the Republic of Ireland and 14 per cent in Northern Ireland profess to have no religious allegiance. This category includes agnostics, atheists and Humanists. Their number has grown slightly in the last few decades. The remainder of the population is divided between three distinguishable groups: those belonging to smaller Protestant denominations, such as the Methodists (recognised as the fourth largest denomination in Ireland), Baptists, Congregationalists, Free Presbyterians, and the Christian Brethren; a tiny minority belonging to New Religious Movements; and finally a small number of individuals who belong to one of the major world religions – Jews and Muslims chiefly.

(The beliefs and practices of some of the Churches and religious groups mentioned in this section are expanded upon in later chapters).

Religious trends in Ireland

The twentieth century was a period of unprecedented change in Western society: the spread of democracy; rising levels of education and wealth; two world wars that underlined the dangers of totalitarianism; the questioning of traditional authorities; and increasing political co-operation across Europe. The Churches have not been immune from these developments as well as having to respond to shifts of meaning and significance in their own understanding of the nature of Christianity. The relative geographical isolation of Ireland on the periphery of Europe and its neutrality throughout two world wars has meant that the influences that have shaped the rest of Europe have not been experienced as forcefully here as elsewhere. But this is not to say that society has not changed and evolved and this in turn has required the Churches to evolve and adapt. In this section we will consider three different religious trends in Ireland. The first is that of secularisation, which draws attention to changing patterns of religious expression and a degree of disenchantment with traditional institutional religion. Such disenchantment is in fact reflected in the second trend that we consider, that is, the rise of the Charismatic movement. Its influence on the mainline Christian Churches may be less than it was a decade ago, but its influence continues and arguably has become greater as witnessed by the growth of house churches and fellowship churches across Ireland, North and South. The attraction of Charismatic Christianity illustrates the quest for authentic Christian experience and is part of a wider movement within society that accentuates personal fulfilment and individualism. Finally, we look briefly at Irish ecumenism and the trend towards increasing co-operation among the mainline Churches.

Secularisation

Traditionally secularisation is defined as the decline of the social significance of religion. To this is often added the further clause that it also refers to a decline in individual religious belief and practice. The introduction by the state of a law permitting divorce or the decriminalisation of homosexuality in certain contexts would be examples of secularisation in the first sense. Falling numbers of individuals (as a percentage of the population as a whole) attending church or being confirmed would be examples of secularisation in the second sense. There has been a decline in religion in both senses in most countries in Western Europe. England and Wales are particularly clear examples. The situation in Ireland is more ambiguous. Religion remains significant at the level of participation and of personal belief. Surveys indicate that there are high levels of church attendance; very high levels of belief in God; and very low levels of those who describe themselves as agnostics or atheists. Among Catholics there remains significant support for traditional Church teaching: the majority of the Catholic population believe that hell exists; that extra-marital sex is always wrong; and that homosexual relations are sinful. Interestingly, levels of religious participation and levels of support for traditional Catholic moral teaching are slightly higher in the North that in the South of Ireland. On the basis of public measures of religiosity Ireland and Poland are the most religious countries in Europe. Religious commitment and practice remain high in most parts of Ireland, despite predictions by some social theorists in the nineteen-sixties and the nineteen-seventies that religion would decline markedly towards the end of the twentieth century. There are exceptions to this picture of buoyant religion in Ireland: mass attendance is in decline in some less-economically favoured areas within the larger cities and more broadly across Dublin.

How far do the considerations we have reviewed lead us to conclude that secularisation is not a major force or trend within Irish society? There are reasons for being cautious. Even though the population as a whole continues to affirm and to practise Christian faith, there are concerns. For example, religious adherence to Christianity in the North of Ireland is strong, but we also know from other conflict situations that religion acts as a focus of identity and, as the differences between communities lessen as conflicts are resolved, so religion declines in importance. In the context of Northern Ireland it may well be that commitment to Catholicism is in part an attempt to unify and consolidate opposition to those who are perceived as representing a different culture and ethos. Religion acts as a public badge of opposition to 'British' rule. On this reading, commitment to Catholicism in Northern Ireland is, among other things, an expression of Irish nationalism. A beleaguered group, and until recently the Catholic community has felt beleaguered (ironically it now seems that it is Protestants who feel beleaguered and insecure) uses religion to reinforce its identity over against other identities that are regarded as alien and threatening. If there is truth in this interpretation, then one would expect that as the current peace process develops and the different communities grow closer together so the use of religion to reinforce difference (on both sides) will diminish and consequently support for religion will decline. The idea that religious allegiance is stronger in conflict situations is also due to the fact that religion provides spiritual resources on which people can draw. This feature of religion is also presumably a factor in the high levels of religiosity in Northern Ireland. Again as the 'conflict' diminishes so one may anticipate a falling off in commitment. Such explanations, however, do not explain the high levels of religious participation in the South of Ireland. But do high levels of religious participation reveal the full story? There is evidence that although support for religion remains strong, it is much less strong among the younger generation than the older generation: this is particularly true of urban young people. This suggests that the process of secularisation has begun and that as time advances so its significance will increase and become more widely recognised. There is also the issue of the effects of religion upon people. People may attend church and identify with religion but do they live their lives according to religious standards? Can we assume because most people go to church that Christian teaching is followed by the majority of people? There is some evidence that suggests otherwise. Increasing numbers of individuals seeking divorce and surveys that reveal widespread sexual activity outside marriage can be cited as evidence that despite church attendance commitment to Church teaching is in decline. Equally, many of the younger generation seem to combine public profession of Christianity with scepticism regarding many features of traditional Catholic teaching. Does this mean that the younger generation is becoming less religious or simply expressing their religious convictions in a different way?

We introduced this section by defining secularisation as the declining social significance of religion and if this definition is followed then there is clear evidence that the process of secularisation is well advanced in Irish society. Increasingly the state and public institutions have moved away from affirming and reinforcing specifically Catholic moral teaching. The Irish state in the last two decades has moved away from enshrining Catholicism in social legislation. Recent scandals in the Church have diminished its moral authority and have advanced the case for the state to be religiously neutral on matters of public policy and morality. This has resulted in the increasing privatisation of religious belief and as such this is usually regarded as evidence of secularisation in the straightforward sense that religion is losing *social* influence. Certainly Catholicism still enjoys a privileged formal status within the state and this is accentuated on state occasions but this status translates into diminishing political and social influence.

The Charismatic movement
The *World Christian Encyclopedia* records the rise of the Charismatic movement within the Catholic Church in the following statistics: in 1970 there were about half a million people involved in Catholic Renewal prayer groups at least once in a monthly period; by 2000 there were 160,000 such groups and over 19 million people involved at least once in the month. Before turning to the situation in Ireland we will look

briefly at the rise of the Charismatic movement and note its distinctive theology.

The roots of Charismatic Christianity lie in Classical Pentecostalism, which emerged in the U.S.A. at the turn of the Century. It was on 1st January 1901 that Agnes Ozman had hands laid on her at the Bible School of Charles F. Parnham in Topeka, Kansas, after which she began to 'speak in tongues' and experienced what would soon be called 'baptism of the Spirit'. Those who were open to charismatic gifts of the Spirit, such as speaking in tongues, prophecy, healings, and words of knowledge, were not accepted by mainstream Protestant Churches, and as a consequence Pentecostal Churches came into being: the name 'Pentecostal' is derived from the Day of Pentecost when the early Church received the Spirit and the disciples 'spoke in tongues'. By the 1960s the mainline Protestant Churches had begun to be influenced by Pentecostalism and there emerged a new interest in appropriated the experience of the gifts, but without the accompanying Pentecostal theology.

By the late 1960s the Charismatic Movement had begun to influence the Catholic Church (the New Testament word for 'gifts' of the Spirit is *charismata*, hence Charismatic movement). The origins of this influence are usually traced to 1967, when two Catholic laymen at Duquesne University attended a Neo-Pentecostal prayer meeting and had hands laid upon them, after which they spoke in tongues. Within a short time there were similar occurrences at Notre Dame, Indiana. At this stage it became appropriate to speak of the Catholic Renewal movement. Within a few years the movement was world wide within the Catholic Church. While many Episcopal conferences warned of the dangers of the movement, their overall evaluation was positive. In a memorable address in 1975, Pope Paul VI described the movement as a 'chance for the Church and the world', a sentiment repeated by John Paul II in 1981. Pope Paul appointed Cardinal Suenens of Belgium to oversee the development of Catholic Renewal. Under Suenens' guidance Charismatic renewal was integrated into Catholic theology and, more importantly, Catholic spirituality.

Although Charismatic Renewal in Ireland began first among Northern Protestants, its influence soon spread to Southern Ireland. In early 1972 at a meeting in Dublin addressed by Rev. Tom Smail, then minister of Whiteabbey Presbyterian Church in Belfast, and Fr. Joe McGeady, an Irish Catholic who working in England, the gifts of the Spirit were experienced by members of the predominantly Catholic audience. Support for the validity of the experience enjoyed by those who attended the meeting came from a number of Catholic priests who had attended charismatic conferences and who had experienced 'baptism of the Spirit' in the United States. By 1974 a national committee of four Catholics and two Protestants was formed to further the case for Charismatic renewal in the Churches. This was a bold ecumenical venture for the times. The ecumenical dimension of Charismatic Renewal was strengthened by the work of the Christian renewal centre at Rostrevor, Co. Down, founder by Rev. Cecil Kerr in 1974. Throughout the seventies the Renewal movement grew throughout Ireland, though particularly among Catholics in the South. In fact at this stage Charismatic renewal became a distinctively Catholic phenomenon in the South, resisted by most of the Protestant Churches. A number of Charismatic Catholic Churches and communities emerged to champion the case for a more experiential form of Catholic Christianity. For example, Fr Tom Tierney and Tom Flynn founded the Light of Christ Community in Dublin, which helped to host a large international Catholic Charismatic conference in 1978 and for a time produced a monthly magazine entitled *New Creation*, concerned with Charismatic renewal in the Irish Catholic Church. Since the 1980s the Catholic Charismatic Renewal movement in Ireland has lost impetus (though there still exists a group of this name that organises conferences and coordinates prayer services in Catholic dioceses in Ireland), and the numbers involved in 'charismatic' activities within Catholicism has declined, even if it remains an important aspect of Irish Catholic Christian experience. But of course Charismatic renewal is not confined to the Catholic Church and the last two decades have seen the emergence across Ireland, particularly in urban areas, of independent fellowships and house churches. Many of these groups simply prefer to describe themselves as Christian rather than Catholic or Protestant. In their view such historical labels have become divisive and obstruct the progress of God's kingdom.

Ecumenism
We have noted the influence of the Charismatic renewal movement in bringing Christians of different traditions (and from different parts of Ireland) together and in fostering a sense of fellowship between them. In a sense this is ecumenism at a practical and experiential level. Its significance should not be diminished. It also illustrates the point that the subject of ecumenism should not be confined to official Church relations and formal meetings between clergy of different traditions. Much ecumenism goes unnoticed when Christian of various commitments meet and talk about their faith and reflect upon their similarities and differences. Equally, ecumenism is a movement within the different Churches as they seek to improve formal relations with each other and to bear witness to the unity that Christians enjoy in Christ. It is to the formal aspects of ecumenism that we turn.

The noun 'ecumenism' and the adjective 'ecumenical' are derived from the Greek word *'oikoumene'*, which means 'the whole inhabited world'. Gradually, the term came to refer to the whole Church and that which unites the Church, for example, ecumenical creeds are those creeds that were formulated before divisions in the Church occurred or creeds whose truth is accepted by all Christians. Building on this usage, ecumenism has come to designate the modern Christian movement concerned with the unity and mission of the Church. The modern ecumenical movement began within Protestantism in the first decades of the twentieth century, when interdenominational cooperation in missionary activity and fellowship through the Student Christian Movement created a climate that led to the establishment of international conferences concerned with theological, social, and political issues. In 1948 the main Protestant denominations came together to form the World Council of Churches. Catholic ecumenism is usually dated from the 1960s: in 1960 the Archbishop of Canterbury, Geoffrey Fisher (1887–1972), visited Pope John XXIII (1881–1963) in Rome and in the next year the Vatican sent official observers to the third assembly of the World Council of Churches. Non-Catholic representatives were invited as observers to attend the Second Vatican Council. In the Decree on Ecumenism issued in 1964, members of other Christian communions are described as 'separated brethren' rather than as being outside the Church. This positive overture resulted in much warmer relations between Catholicism, Eastern Orthodoxy and the different denominations of Protestantism. From this date there has been a series of conversations and agreements between the Catholic Church and other Christian communions.

The genesis of the modern ecumenical movement in Ireland may be dated to the establishment in 1906 by the Presbyterian and Methodist Churches of a joint committee to promote united approaches. In 1910 the Presbyterian Church and the Church of Ireland agreed to cooperate in a similar way. These initiatives led to the creation in 1923 of the United Council of Christian Churches and Religious Communions in Ireland, a body that in 1966 changed its name to the Irish Council of Churches (ICC). The member Churches are Anglican, Presbyterian, Lutheran, Methodist, Non-Subscribing Presbyterian, Moravian, Greek Orthodox, the Religious Society of Friends and the Salvation Army. Official observers of the Catholic and Coptic Orthodox Churches attend major meetings. For a quarter of a century the ICC in conjunction with the Catholic Church's Commission for Justice and Peace has promoted peace and reconciliation in Northern Ireland. These two groups, for instance, sponsor a peace-education programme in schools. The most noteworthy ecumenical initiative of their joint work has been the Inter-Church Committee, which has met every eighteen months or so, usually at Ballymacscanlon, near Dundalk, since 1973. At these meetings dialogue has taken place on a great many areas of common interest and theological concern, subjects such as Church, scripture and authority, sectarianism and the Churches' contribution to peace and justice. The fruit of this on-going dialogue is reflected in the production of a number of inter-church reports and publications: booklets on *Ecumenical Principles, Reading the Bible Together, Marriage and the Family in Ireland Today*, and *Freedom, Justice and Responsibility in Ireland Today* have been produced. The ICC and representatives of the Catholic Hierarchy have also produced reports on social problems, for example, drug abuse and the use of alcohol among young people.

At a national level, regular meetings take place between the leaders of the four main Churches in Ireland (Catholic, Anglican, Presbyterian and Methodist); and, at local level, contact is maintained by interested clergy and laity. Each year a week of prayer for Christian Unity is held. A number of different groups and organisation within the Churches work to further the cause of ecumenism and to improve community relations, marred as they have been by sectarian division and communal violence. Such groups include the Irish School of Ecumenics, founded in 1970, the Columbanus, Corrymeela, and Lamb of God communities, Protestant and Catholic Encounter (PACE), and the Christian Renewal Centre at Rostrevor. The theological motivation of ecumenism is Christ's words in John's Gospel that his followers would 'all be one'. The Christocentric nature of Christian ecumenism is stressed in the New Testament: the closer we come to Christ the closer we come to each other.

1.2   PRIMAL RELIGION

Primal Religion, as the term suggests, refers to the earliest manifestations of religion in human culture and history. What were the original religious impulses from which current religions have evolved? The earliest evidence of religious belief can tentatively be traced to archaeological remains that reveal our ancient ancestors to have taken care over the disposal of the dead. This suggests that they had a belief that there was some form of existence after death. The dead were buried with implements such as weapons and tools that might have a possible use in a post-mortem existence. A concern with the burial of the dead is found across different ancient civilisations, the Celts and the Egyptians, for example. Many of these early burial sites also pointed the body along an east-west axis that probably indicates some relationship to the movement of the sun. There are those who suggest that the sun may have originally been worshipped as the god of life and harvest. Such associations are natural: it is the sun that brings life to the soil and produces the harvest. Other evidence of possible religious ideas held by our earliest human ancestors comes from cave art. Some scholars interpret cave paintings of animals wounded by arrows as linked to magical rites that were undertaken before a hunt for food to ensure success. Characteristic features of Primal Religion include a strong belief in spirits; sacrifice as a means of propitiating the spirits or of gaining benefits from them; and the existence of gods and lesser deities who related to different aspects of life and the agricultural year.

The relationship of Primal Religion to currently existing forms of Traditional Religion is a controversial question within the study of religion. It was fashionable at the end of the nineteenth century and the beginning of the twentieth century to read off the details of Primal Religion from the religions of geographically isolated indigenous tribes who were presumed to have retained their ancient customs and traditions. On this basis the religious of the Australian Aborigines or the beliefs of the North American Plains Indians were simply equated with the earliest form of religion. There are difficulties with this strategy, as with the motivation that frequently underlay it, namely the quest to fit the facts of religion into an evolutionary framework. The chief difficulty is that there is considerable variety of belief and practice within existing indigenous religious groups. How do we decide which group preserves the original version of religion? Scholars are now much more cautions about facilely equating Primal Religion with contemporary Tribal Religion. Nevertheless, some aspects of contemporary Tribal Religion clearly parallel the beliefs and practices of Primal Religion as these have been revealed to archaeological and historical research. For this reason it may be useful for readers to become acquainted with the section on African Traditional Religion in Chapter 9. This provides an overall orientation to some of the parallels that exist between African Traditional Religion and the world of Primal Religion. A reading of this will provide the necessary context for an appreciation of the discussion that follows on some central concepts of Primal Religion.

Mana

'Mana' is a word of Melanesian origin, meaning 'supernatural power'. Accordingly it may be defined as an impersonal force or power thought to reside in certain persons, objects or places, making them powerful and even dangerous. It was introduced into the study of religion by R. R. Marett, in connection with his theory of pre-animism or animatism. Marett's contention was that prior to 'belief in spiritual

beings', i.e. animism, which writers such as E. B. Taylor
(1832–1917) and many others of the period regarded as the
earliest stage in the evolution of religion, there was, in fact, an
earlier pre-animist stage from which animism descended. The
defining feature of this earlier stage of religion was human
recognition of the existence of an 'impersonal supernatural
power' that attached itself to objects and persons. For a time,
Marett's theory enjoyed some degree of scholarly support.
The roots of religion can be traced to our earliest ancestors'
experience of an uncanny power that simultaneously attracted
and repelled them. From this ambiguous experience, it was
contended, the edifice of religion came to be built. More
critically, what our ancestors sensed as 'uncanny', modern men
such as Marett could now rationalise and explain in scientific
terms: the origin of religion lay in some psychological
mechanism or instinctive reaction within the human self and
not in some purported revelation from an external deity.

Ironically, Marett's theory soon broke on the altar of
scientific truth. He had appropriated the term 'mana' and its
meaning from R. H. Codrington's nineteenth-century study of
the Melanesian people, but unfortunately he missed
Codrington's qualifications and nuances of interpretation.
Mana, for the Melanesians, as described by Codrington, might
well take the form of an impersonal power, but more
characteristically it was the manifestation of a spirit's presence
and power. Marett's suggestion of a pre-animist stage of
religion was discredited. Primal religion could indeed speak of
uncanny powers and feelings, but behind such powers lay the
world of the spirits.

Tabu
'Tabu' is a word of Polynesian origin that has come to be used
in the study of religion to denote anything set apart,
consecrated and therefore inappropriate for ordinary use.
Broadly speaking, any person, object or place through which

the spirit world expresses itself has potentially the quality of mana (see above) and as a consequence is subject to tabu.

The supernatural power that the spirits possess can be communicated to persons, especially kings, chiefs and priests, namely, those who are dedicated to the service of the spirits or gods. They mediate the spirit's power and act as guardians of the divine order. Persons who mediate and channel the power (mana) of the spirits are set apart as different and therefore the rules of interaction with them are narrowly drawn to acknowledge this difference: they may not be approached directly or touched by the common people. A person, place or thing that is tabu is hedged by restrictions and rules of contact. Similarly, a cult-centre (a place where worship, say sacrifice and offerings are conducted) is tabu because it is the place in which the spirits communicate with men and women; cult objects – images, instruments, symbols – are likewise tabu and can only be handled under the supervision of those who are ritually pure. Paradoxically, contact with tabu objects or persons cannot be entirely excluded, for if this were to happen the tabu items would become entirely inaccessible and therefore of no human or religious interest. As a consequence, a series of rules are devised to make the holy power in some sense accessible, while simultaneously preserving its 'otherness'. The rules of tabu fall into two categories. There are rules that restrict and govern access to sacred persons and objects, and there are rules that detail certain kinds of actions and activity as ritually unclean or 'polluted'. To break the rules of tabu is to face the possibility of attracting the wrath of the spirits. In such cases ritual incantations or sacrifices may be necessary if sickness or danger is to be avoided.

Totem

The Ojibwa word 'totem' was first used in the West in the late eighteenth century to refer to belief in a 'favourite animal spirit' among North American Indians. Some tribes believed themselves to stand in a special relationship to certain animals, birds or even plants. A group or tribe might take the name of an animal or bird for themselves and would not normally kill or eat it. An individual might also have a personal totem or 'guardian spirit' in either animal or bird form. Totems were treated with great respect and the spirit that was believed to inhabit them was to be worshipped. It was later noted by anthropologists that Australian Aborigines entertained the same belief in totems.

What is the explanation for totems? Why do tribes revere and worship totems? One possible answer is that worship of totems may indicate a deep-seated respect for nature and the natural world. The uncertainties of food and the need to survive in a hostile and uncompromising environment may have produced a sense of human vulnerability before the natural world. This sense may have expressed itself in some kind of acknowledgement of the need to respect nature and this is symbolised in respect and worship of some particular species of animal or bird. A further answer might be that the tribe aspires to possess the same characteristics as the totem – the bird that soars effortlessly above the earth and strikes terror into its prey serves as a model for the tribe to emulate.

Shaman

The word 'shaman' is of northern Asiatic origin and means a 'priest' or 'medicine man'. Shamanism is properly used to describe the indigenous religion of northern Eurasia, but is also now used to refer to a type of Primal Religion in which certain features, chiefly sacred trance and the control of spirits, are prominent. A shaman is a medium between the visible world and the invisible spirit world; he practises magic and communicates with the spirits and the spirit world for purposes of healing, divination, and control over 'natural' events. Shamanism is based on belief in spirits (animism), whose presence and action influence nature and human affairs. The shaman protects humans from destructive spirits by rendering the spirits harmless.

Shamans have to undergo a long period of intensive training in order to fit them for their role as mediators between the human world and the world of the spirits. By following a rigorous programme of ascetic exercises and by perfecting the means of entering into trance states, shamans are believed to gain supernatural powers. These powers involve being able to contact and enter the world of the spirits with safety. Typically, a shaman identifies himself with a particular spirit who acts on his behalf in the spirit world and who is his source of authority over other spirits. An elaborate rite of initiation is carried out in which the shaman receives and declares his power over the spirits; special clothes are subsequently worn to distinguish the shaman from others. One of the most important elements of the Shaman's equipment is his drum, which is used to summon the spirits. The shaman mediates with the spirits on behalf of his tribe and on behalf of individuals. He offers sacrifices, interprets the will of the gods and spirits and cures disease by the use of special charms and chants. In a state of trace he dispatches his spirit into the spirit world and interacts with other spirits, and on occasions he engages in combat with malevolent spirits in order to remove a curse or to cure someone from illness.

The influence of the concepts of mana, tabu, and shamanism can be seen in the major world religions. Most of the major religions, although subordinating the world of the spirits to God, still retain belief in the existence of spirits. Chinese religion places a strong emphasis upon rituals supporting the spirits of ancestors and Catholic Christianity accepts that those beyond death can benefit from appropriately performed rituals. The great religions all speak of evil spirits who can influence events on earth and who wage war upon God and his servants. Special services can be conducted in all religions to ward off evil powers and influences. The concept of tabu is also found within the great world religions. In Catholic Christianity there are rules governing how one should approach the sacrament of Mass, there are rules in relation to the host, and so on. One might even argue that the priestly rule of celibacy is a tabu rule, designed to preserve the 'sacredness' and 'otherness' of the priesthood. Finally, the role of the shaman in Primal Religion provides fruitful parallels to the role of religious officials in a number of the world religions. Many of the religions restrict access to the divine and accord a central role to the work of special 'religious' individuals. One thinks here of the role of the Catholic priest in the celebration of Mass and in the sacrament of Reconciliation or the role of the Brahmin priest in Hinduism, for only he can conduct certain ceremonies and dispense certain blessings. There are many other examples of parallels between the central concepts of Primal Religion and contemporary religious belief and practice. Our discussion is intended as illustrative; subsequent chapters will provide further material from which parallels can be drawn.

1.3   THE HOLY

In the West we tend to associate holiness with the Judaeo-Christian tradition and for this reason we will begin by reviewing use of the word 'holiness' in the Hebrew Bible and the Christian New Testament. The word for holiness in Hebrew is 'Kaddosh', the root meaning of which is 'that which is separate'. Hence the meaning of holiness is that which is set apart for sacred or religious use. Anything closely associated with God is holy. Hence in the Hebrew Bible, such things as garments, vessels, and places that are associated with God and worship of him are regarded as holy. The priest is also considered holy and of course God embodies holiness. In its original use the word holy did not necessarily carry any moral connotations, but as religion evolved and developed so holiness came to acquire such connotations. 'Be you holy as I am Holy', was God's summons to Israel. Certainly this means that the people of Israel had to separate themselves from the beliefs and practices of the surrounding nations, but by the stage these words were written, they also meant that God's people had to practise righteousness and pursue justice in emulation of the perfect righteousness and justice of God. The word translated as 'saints' in the Christian New Testament essentially means 'holy ones'. The Apostle Paul regards all those who follow Christ and are members of the Church as saints: they are separate from the world and called to distinguish themselves from others by acts of love.

The idea of individuals and things set apart for religious use is not unique to Judaism and Christianity. It is arguably present in all the religions. (Whether the Jewish and Christian moral connotations of holiness are present in the different religions is a much more controversial issue). For many scholars of religion holiness is the defining feature of religion. This viewpoint is chiefly indebted to the work of the German theologian and historian of religion, Rudolf Otto.

In *The Idea of the Holy* (1917) Otto argues that experience of the Holy is central to religion. He wrote originally in German using the term *'das heilig'*, which was translated into English as 'the Holy'. It should be noted, however, that *das heilig* could equally be translated into English as 'the sacred'. The translator of Otto had to make a choice and chose *holy*, but some other writers, such as Mircea Eliade, prefer to speak of 'the Sacred'. As a consequence use of either terminology usually reveals a debt to Otto and his interpretation of religion. Otto's central point is that religious experience is mysterious and ineffable (basically non-rational). Religious experience is different from all other experiences; and this is because the object of experience, the Holy, is different from all other objects. Otto developed a distinctive terminology in order to express his ideas. He wanted to challenge the theologians of his day, whom he believed had 'domesticated' the idea of God. God for them was the supremely rational principle who ordered the world and the Church along rational and predictable lines. Otto believed that such a view falsified the true nature of religion, which instead witnessed to the existence of a mysterious or numinous power before which men stood mute in awe. Experience of the Holy (the Numinous) defies classification and literal description. In an attempt to underline the mysterious nature of the Holy, he used the Latin phrase *'mysterium tremendum et fascinans'* to designate the different components within genuine religious experience. As *mysterium*, the Numinous is 'wholly other' – entirely different from anything we experience in ordinary life. It evokes a reaction of silence. But the Numinous is also a *mysterium tremendum*. It provokes terror because it presents itself as overwhelming power. There is a sense of awfulness (inspiring awe), overpoweringness (inspiring a feeling of humility), and energy (creating an impression of immense vigour) in the presence of 'numinous power'. Finally, the Numinous presents itself as *fascinans*, as merciful and gracious. The Numinous is that which is holy, that which is separate and transcendent and instils in the worshipper a sense both of inadequacy and dependency. Otto writes that 'The deepest and most fundamental element in all strong and sincerely felt religious emotion,' is to be found, 'in strong, sudden ebullitions of personal piety, ... in the fixed and ordered solemnities of rites and liturgies, and again in the atmosphere that clings to old religious monuments and buildings, to temples and to churches.' The subject of experience of the Holy is enraptured, transported into a transcendent world beyond the ordinary world and objects of space and time. This sense of the Holy is so intense, according to Otto, that it underlines the contrast that exists between the world of the sacred and the profane world of everyday existence. The religious person operates on two levels: usually on the profane or everyday level, but with occasional moments or longer periods of access to a higher, sacred level.

The relationship between the sacred and the profane in religion

The sacred is that which is dedicated or set aside for religious use, and as such commands worship or reverence. By contrast the profane is that which is not religious, the world of the ordinary and the mundane. In *The Idea of the Holy* Otto identified and discussed this distinction, but his account at this point has been much less influential than his account of the nature of experience of the Holy. A much more important discussion of the distinction between the sacred and the profane is to be found in Emil Durkheim's *The Elementary Forms of the Religious Life* (1912). Durkheim defined religion as 'a unified system of beliefs and practices relative to sacred things set apart and forbidden.' The contrast between the sacred and the profane is central to his thought: in more recent literature the contrast is often expressed as that between the sacred and the secular.

The sacred can take many forms. There are sacred things, sacred ceremonies and sacred places. Here are some examples of each.

- Sacred Things and Places: a river (Ganges); a book (the Hebrew Bible, the Qur'an, the Bhagavad Gita); an object (an altar or crucifix or relic in Catholic Christianity; an icon in Eastern Orthodoxy); a place (Bethlehem, Mecca, Amritsar, Rome); a day or period of time (Easter, Divali, Eid, Passover); an object or animal (a cow in Hinduism).
- Sacred Ceremonies: these bring people together for community activity. They may involve singing and dancing, prayer and ritual, bowing and performing religious actions such as lighting sacred candles and reciting sacred words.

Sacred things are necessarily set apart as superior, powerful, forbidden to normal contact and deserving of worship or great respect. Profane things are the opposite: they belong to the ordinary and the mundane things of life. The overwhelming concern of religion, according to Durkheim, is with the first of these two sets of things. But why are things sacred? Durkheim had a controversial answer to this question. He believes that things are sacred because they provide a focus for community loyalty. The sacred binds individuals together to form a moral community. The sacred creates a sense of community and in this way brings people together for the common good. Durkheim's view is that religion serves noble purposes as it mobilises bonds of affection and unites people in common tasks and purposes. The essence of religion is the creation of community. Ultimately, for him, devotion to the sacred is devotion to the group to which one belongs. The realm of the sacred does not require a supernatural justification. Religious activity is as an expression of group loyalty. Whether God or the Holy exists is almost entirely irrelevant to the practice of religion. It is unlikely that such an interpretation will satisfy religious people. In their view the realm of the sacred is the realm of God's revelation and action. Things are sacred because they are used by holy individuals or for a sacred purpose. People are sacred because they speak on behalf of God or act as a mediator between the people and God, or because they radiate the divine presence, and so on.

There is little doubt that Durkheim's distinction between the sacred and the profane provides an interesting perspective on the nature of religion. One can, for example, use it to illuminate the concept of secularisation. It could be argued that in the process of secularisation the realm of the sacred contracts as the items within it are gradually incorporated into the realm of the profane. The notion of marriage as a religious covenant is replaced in society with the notion of marriage as a purely legal agreement: religious institutions, such as schools and hospitals, give up their religious affiliation and continue as secular institutions. Such an interpretation provides an illuminating vista on the nature and character of religious change in society. Furthermore, Durkheim's idea that the sacred does not require a supernatural reference or focus offers an interesting perspective on the evolving nature of religious expression. One could contend that the category of the sacred is as important and influential in society as it once was. There may have been a decline in church attendance, which some may interpret as a decline in influence of the sacred, but equally it could be argued that the number of people who either watch or attend sporting fixtures has increased and that their behaviour is analogous to religious worship. It is not that interest in the sacred is in decline only that it has found a different focus.

Durkheim's idea that the concept of the sacred has an application whether or not there is a supernatural realm of existence has meet with some opposition from scholars of religion. In reaction Mircea Eliade, in a book entitled *The Sacred and the Profane* (1957), while upholding a distinction between the sacred and the profane, argued that the category of the sacred is irreducibly religious in the sense that the sacred witnesses to the existence of a supernatural realm of existence. The sacred has an application to reality not because people choose to regard some things as sacred but because there is a sacred reality that manifests itself to people. Eliade used the word 'hierophany' to refer to human encounters with the sacred.

The contrasting interpretations of the nature of the sacred advanced by Durkheim and Eliade are illustrative of a more fundamental debate in the scholarly study of religion. Durkheim's account is agnostic with regard to the truth of religion, whereas Eliade's account acknowledges the truth of religion, more precisely, it seems to acknowledge the truth of each and every religion. Which approach, if either, is appropriate to the study of religion? Should the study of religion simply report and describe religious beliefs and practices or should it attempt to penetrate more deeply into the truth of religion? There is much that could be said on these matters, and thankfully it is not our task to provide answers. What is to be hoped, however, is that the material brought together in this study will provide the means by which a more informed decision can be made on the truth or otherwise of religion.

2

Judaism

Hear, O Israel, the Lord is our God, the Lord is one. You shall love the Lord your God with all your heart, and with all your soul, and with all your might. Keep these words that I am commanding you today in your heart.

(Deuteronomy 6:4-6)

Judaism is a religion whose significance far exceeds what would be expected from the number of its adherents. Its influence is particularly strong on Christianity, which has incorporated the Hebrew Bible into its canon of Sacred Scripture. The central ideas of Christianity, and Islam as well, are derived from the Jewish tradition.

An overview of Judaism

God

Jews believe that there is a single God who not only created the universe, but with whom every Jew can have an individual and personal relationship. God is a God of history and he has chosen to have a special relationship with the Jewish people; he has entered into a covenant relationship with them. God is faithful and acts to vindicate and lead his people, and in return his covenant people worship him and keep his holy laws. The Jews seek to bring holiness into every aspect of their lives.

One of the primary expressions of Jewish faith is that God is one. This is affirmed twice daily by devout Jews when they recite a compilation of passages, referred to as the Shema, from the Torah: it begins, 'Hear [*Shema*], O Israel, the Lord is our God, the Lord is one.' This simple statement expresses a number of important Jewish ideas about God – there is only one God, and he is Lord and Creator of the universe. God is also regarded by Jews as all-powerful (omnipotent), all-knowing (omniscient), present everywhere (omnipresent), and eternal. God is essentially good. Judaism has always maintained that God's justice is tempered by mercy; the two qualities are perfectly balanced. Although the Scriptures speak of various parts of God's body, such as the hand of God, and speak of God in anthropomorphic terms, such as God walking in the Garden of Eden, Judaism firmly maintains that God is a living spirit, without a body. Any reference to God's body is simply a figure of speech, a means of making God's actions more comprehensible to beings living in a material world. God is not to be represented in physical form; to do such is considered idolatry. According to one ancient tradition the sin of the Golden Calf incident, when the people made an image, while waiting for Moses to come down from Mount Sinai, was not that they had chosen another deity, but that they tried to represent God in a physical form.

Torah

God did not just appear to the Jews, he gave them instructions concerning how to live. These instructions are contained in the Torah and the oral traditions collected in the Mishnah.

Torah means 'instruction'. Jews use the word in a number of ways. Sometimes they mean the first five books of the Hebrew Bible and sometimes they mean the whole of the Hebrew Bible, i.e. those that make up the Christian 'Old Testament' (the

books that Christians call the New Testament are not part of
Jewish scripture). The Hebrew Bible is known as the written
Torah. It is divided into three parts: Torah, the Five Books of
Moses; Nevi'im, the Books of the Prophets; and Ketuvim, Holy
Writings. The initial Hebrew letters of the three sections make
up the word Tenach. This is the name Jews give to the Bible. It
is mostly written in Hebrew, with a few sections written in
Aramaic. Hand written copies on parchment scrolls are used in
the synagogue. Individuals are not supposed to touch the
scrolls; some say because they are too holy; some say because
the parchment, made from animal skins, is a source of ritual
defilement. Instead, the reader follows the text with a pointer
called a *Yad*. Yad means 'hand' in Hebrew, and the pointer
usually is in the shape of a hand with a pointing index finger.
The scrolls are kept covered with fabric, and often ornamented
with silver crowns on the handles of the scrolls and a silver
breastplate on the front.

In addition to the written scriptures, Jews also speak of the
'Oral Torah', which contains traditions explaining what the
scriptures mean and how to interpret and apply the Laws.
Orthodox Jews believe God taught the Oral Torah to Moses, and
he taught it to others, down to the present day. This tradition was
maintained in oral form until about the second century CE,
when the oral law was brought together and written down in a
document called the Mishnah. Over the next few centuries,
additional commentaries elaborating on the Mishnah were
written down in Jerusalem and Babylon. These additional
commentaries are known as the Gemara. The Gemara and the
Mishnah together are known as the Talmud. This was completed
in the fifth century CE. Jews interpret their Scriptures in the light
of the interpretations collected in the Talmud.

Covenant
Jews understand their relationship with God in terms of a
covenant, that is, in terms of an agreement between them and

God. The Hebrew Bible describes how God made a covenant with Abraham. God chose Abraham to be the father of a people who would be special to him, and who in return would worship and honour him. The story of the Jews is the story of God's continuing relationship with the Jews and their faithfulness to him. In the patriarchal period God guided the Jewish people through many troubles, and at the time of Moses he gave them a set of rules by which they should live, including the Ten Commandments. This was the beginning of Judaism as a structured religion. Over the centuries Judaism developed and evolved in response to God's call to obedience and to the changing circumstances and situations in which that obedience was effected.

Varieties of Judaism

Jews are divided according to their beliefs and practices and according to their racial origins, as either having roots in central Europe (Ashkenazi Jews) or Spain and the Middle East (Sephardi Jews). There are a number of divisions within Judaism. We will confine our attention to Orthodox and Reform Judaism.

Orthodox Judaism

Orthodox Jews are those who follow the original teachings and traditions of the faith closely. Although the word 'Orthodox', literally means 'right doctrine', its application to Judaism is better understood as referring to 'right *practice*' rather than doctrine. Jews believe that the Torah and the Talmud were given by God directly to the Jewish People, and so they regard these documents as being God's actual words and of the highest authority in determining the character and laws of Judaism. The focus of Orthodox Judaism is on observing the teaching of the Torah (written and oral). It aims to be faithful to God and to keep his commandments. Some 613 commandments have been identified in the Torah, though those that relate to worship in the Temple in Jerusalem are not now applicable. Orthodox Jews are the biggest group in most countries outside the USA (where Reform Judaism predominates), e.g. England and Ireland.

Some writers also speak of Ultra-Orthodox Judaism. Ultra-Orthodox Jews stress not only the demands of the oral and written Torah, but also the values and practices of Jews in the later Middle Ages. Traditional Jewish dress and hairstyles associated with this period of Jewish European history are adopted; and religious laws are interpreted very strictly. Ultra-Orthodox Jews live in separate communities and follow their own customs. To some extent they keep apart from the world around them. Ultra-Orthodoxy is one of the fastest growing movements within Judaism.

'Ultra-Orthodox' or 'fundamentalist' are not terms that Jews themselves use, instead they refer to a particular Ultra-Orthodox group, for there are a number of such groups. One of the most important of these groups is Hasidic (or Chasidic) Judaism. The essential elements of it are the significance given to mysticism rather than learning, and the reverence given to the leader of each its of many sects.

Reform Judaism
Reform Jews have adapted their faith and customs to modern life, and incorporated the results of modern biblical scholarship into their interpretation of Judaism. The Reform movement began in Germany in the early nineteenth century. It does not regard the Torah and Talmud as the actual words of God, but as words written by human beings inspired by God. Reform Jews believe that, because the words of these texts were not directly given by God, they can be reinterpreted to suit the conditions of a particular time and place. So, for example, men and women can sit together in a Reform synagogue; in an Orthodox synagogue they would be segregated. In addition, women have a much more prominent role and are able to

participate in services; some women are rabbis and girls celebrate bat mitzvah. A particular feature of Reform Judaism is a strong belief in the importance of creating a just society, and many Reform Jews have been in the forefront of political activism.

2.1   A VISION OF SALVATION

On the question of salvation there is considerable diversity of opinion among Jews and Jewish thinkers. In fact some Jews are reluctant to identify a doctrine of salvation in Judaism. There are a number of reasons for this. First, the concept of personal salvation is not central to contemporary Judaism. The focus of Judaism is on community and on the maintenance of the Jewish community. In other words, to categorise Judaism as a religion of salvation misrepresents its nature. Secondly, and following on from the last point, to present Judaism as a religion of salvation is felt by some Jews to invite invidious comparisons with Christianity. Jews are more concerned with practice rather than belief and doctrine. There is room within Judaism for a variety of opinions on the subject of salvation, and one is no less a Jew (and no less a good Jew) for disagreeing with other Jews. Nevertheless, there are certain ideas that seem to reflect the majority opinion in Jewish thought about the subject of salvation.

The Talmud teaches that there are three participants in the formation of every human being: the mother and father, who provide the physical form, and God, who provides the soul, the personality, and the intelligence. It is said that one of God's greatest gifts to humanity is the knowledge that we are his children and created in his image.

> And God created man in his image, in the image of God he created him; male and female he created them. God blessed them and God said to them, 'Be fertile and

increase, fill the earth and master it, and rule the fish of the sea, the birds of the sky, and all the living things that creep on the earth.

(Genesis 1:27-28)

We are not created in the physical image of God, because Judaism steadfastly maintains that God does not have a body. A Jewish sage, Rashi, contended that we are like God in that we have the ability to understand and discern our place in the world as bearers of God's image: we have a moral and spiritual nature that finds fulfilment in God. Each person is created for fellowship with God, though we have the freedom to rebel and reject communion with God.

In Genesis 2:7, the Bible states that God 'formed' (*vayyitzer*) man. This is an unusual word in Hebrew and the rabbis interpret it to mean that humanity was formed with two impulses: a good impulse (the *yetzer tov*) and an evil impulse (the *yetzer ra*). The yetzer tov is the moral conscience, the inner voice that reminds you of God's law when you consider doing something that is forbidden. According to some teachers of Judaism, it does not enter a person until his thirteenth birthday, when a person becomes responsible for following the commandments. The yetzer ra is more difficult to define, because there are many different ideas about it. It is not a simple desire to do evil or to cause harm or pain. Rather, it is usually conceived as our selfish nature, the desire to satisfy personal needs (food, shelter, sex) without regard for the moral consequences of fulfilling those desires. The yetzer ra is not a bad thing in itself. It was created by God, and all things created by God are good. The Talmud notes that without the yetzer ra (the desire to satisfy personal needs), man would not build a house, marry a wife, beget children or conduct business affairs. But the yetzer ra can lead to wrongdoing when it is not controlled by the yetzer tov. There is nothing inherently wrong with hunger, but it can lead you to steal food. There is nothing inherently wrong with sexual desire, but it can lead to sexual misconduct. The yetzer ra is generally seen as something internal to a person, not as an external force acting on a person. People have the ability to choose which impulse to follow: the yetzer tov or the yetzer ra. At the heart of the Jewish understanding of humanity is that men and women are free to obey or disobey God. The Talmud notes that all people are descended from Adam, so no one can blame his wickedness on his ancestry. On the contrary, we have the freedom to make our own choices, and we will be held responsible for the choices we make. Jews do not believe in a doctrine of original sin: each individual is free to choose which moral and religious path to follow.

As a result of human freedom, people choose to do wrong. The original fellowship between humans and God has been seriously distorted by human disobedience. In addition, the effects of sin are evident in society: injustice, violence, pollution of God's world, and so on. Yet God is merciful towards those who do wrong; and if they confess their wrongs to him and ask for forgiveness, he will remove their transgressions and restore their fellowship with him. The process of repentance that leads to salvation is expressed in Psalm 51:3:

> Have mercy upon me, O God, as befits your faithfulness; and in keeping with your abundant compassion, blot out my transgressions.

Shabbat and holy days provide opportunities for Jews to reflect and to rededicate themselves to God. Through participation in the religious life of the community the impulse for good is strengthened as is the commitment to keep God's holy law. Orthodox Jews believe in an after-life where God's company can be enjoyed more intimately than in this life, yet Judaism has never indulged or developed the kind of speculations about the nature of heaven (or hell for that matter)

that are characteristic of certain form of Christian spirituality.
Quite a number of Jews are agnostic about the nature and
existence of an after-life, for them the quest for justice in this
life is of primary importance.

2.2   THE COMMUNITY OF BELIEVERS

From what has already been said it should be clear that a sense
of community is central to Judaism. This sense is nurtured in
the family and reinforced by synagogue attendance and the
collective celebration of key events in Jewish history. There is a
tradition within Judaism that says nobody should celebrate
Shabbat alone. The individualism that is characteristic of
modern Western life contrasts with the social and communal
orientation of Judaism.

There is nothing comparable to the hierarchical structure of
Catholicism within Judaism. Despite its strong focus on
community and relationships within the community it has
always rejected any notion of hierarchical organisation or
indeed any firm distinction between rabbis and other members
of the Jewish community. There is no representative body of
world Jewry and there does not exist anything like a 'synod' of
rabbis with the power to define Judaism or to promulgate
biding laws. There are communal organisations in parts of the
Jewish world, such as the Board of Deputies of British Jews and
the American Jewish Congress, but these are very loose
organisations with no legislative powers.

The majority of Jews are affiliated to a local synagogue. The
leader of the community is a rabbi. He is essentially a teacher of
the law and it is only in recent years that rabbis have taken on
pastoral responsibilities. Of course a rabbi may enjoy a degree
of authority as a spokesperson for his particular community, and
certainly his views are usually accorded respect, but acceptance
of his views is entirely voluntary. He is not a priest and he does
not mediate God's presence or forgiveness. Rabbis do not enjoy

any kind of privileged access of God denied to other Jews. They are elected by the local congregation and are accountable to it. Their authority is that of scholarship and learning. Even Orthodox rabbis who, on the basis of their knowledge of the legal traditions, render binding decisions in Jewish law, may not claim any kind of infallibility; it is open to other Orthodox rabbis to argue against any decision.

Authority in Judaism is the authority of tradition and the consensus that emerges from faithfulness to the tradition. The focus of the community falls on obedience to God's commandments as revealed in the written and oral Torah, and as interpreted by Jewish sages and rabbis down the generations. The notion of interpreting the Scriptures for oneself is incoherent to the Jew. The Scriptures are to be interpreted within the community of faith in the context of a tradition of interpretation where the meaning of sacred texts is revealed to the devout and the committed.

2.3   A CELEBRATING TRADITION

It is natural for those who are religious to attribute religious significance to special events in one's life, and Jews are no exception. The life-cycle events of birth, the passage to adulthood, marriage and death are marked with religious rituals and endowed with religious meaning. Equally, religious people celebrate significant events in the history of their religion. History is particularly important for the Jews, as God is believed to have revealed himself to them in history and to be directing the events of history in fulfilment of his promises to them. The celebration of events in the believer's life and the celebration of events in the history of the Jewish people combine to form a rich tapestry of remembrance, celebration and hope. Rituals, customs and traditions that have been passed down through the generations provide a sense both of continuity with the past and of purpose for the future.

The Jewish calendar is based on the appearance of the new moon every 29–30 days. Festivals are a regular occurrence, some relating events in the agricultural year to God's bounty and provision, such as Sukkot, and others related exclusively to commemorating events in history, such as the Day of Atonement. Shabbat is also regarded as a festival that celebrates God's resting after his creation of the universe. Shabbat begins when the sun sets on Friday evening and ends at sunset on Saturday. On it devout Jews do not work. A special service called Kiddush, marks the beginning of Shabbat at home. The family comes together to read from the Torah, sing hymns and join together in a special meal. The following morning the family will attend a synagogue service. At the end of Shabbat a further special ceremony, called Havdalah, marks the 'division' between Shabbat and the other days. It is not a division between the sacred and the profane, but rather according a special status to one day in the week is intended to remind us that all days are holy.

Jewish festivals are categorised as either major or minor. Among the latter are Chanukkah, which commemorates the dedication of the Temple, and Purim, which commemorates the events described in the Book of Esther. In the former category are Passover, the Festival of Weeks (Shavuot), Tabernacles (Sukkot), Rejoicing in the law (Simchat Torah) and the Day of Atonement (Yom Kippur). We will look more closely at Passover and the Day of Atonement.

Passover or Pesah commemorates the redemption from slavery and subsequent exodus from Egypt by the Jews in the thirteenth century BCE. God 'passed over' the Jews homes but brought judgement upon the Egyptians. The celebration is over eight days (seven days in Israel) in the month of Nissan, though only the first two and last two days are full-holidays. The middle four days are referred to as *hol ha-Moed* or 'secular days of the holiday' since Jews are permitted to work on these days. Evidence concerning the observance of Passover dates back to the first millennium BCE. During the First and Second Temple periods, Jews were required to sacrifice a paschal lamb or pesah on the evening of the fourteenth of Nissan, the day before Passover began. Historical accounts reveal that many Jews would go to Jerusalem during this time in order to perform this sacrifice. The pesah sacrifice was eliminated, however, after the destruction of the Second Temple.

The importance of the Passover holiday is underlined by the fact that, in accordance with the Torah, it is the only holiday when Jews are required to retell in detail the events to their children. This recounting of the Passover story takes places during the holiday meal or *seder*, which is held on the first two nights of Passover. In Israel and in the Reform tradition, however, the seder is conducted only on the first day. The seder service is conducted in accordance with the Passover *haggadah*, or narration. Near the beginning of the seder, the youngest child asks four questions concerning the meaning of Passover. The adults then respond to these questions by explaining the history and symbolism surrounding the story.

As prescribed in the haggadah, the Passover service contains many rituals. For example, commemoration of the four expressions of redemption in the Book of Exodus, four glasses of wine are typically consumed during the meal. Jews are also required to eat *matzah* or unleavened bread as a reminder of the kind of bread which their forefathers had to eat after they left Egypt in a hurry. Harosset, a mixture of almonds, apples, and wine is consumed as a reminder of the mortar which the Jews used to bind the building bricks together. In addition, it is common for Jews to leave a full cup of wine on the table for Elijah, who is said to be the herald of the Messiah. It is traditional that the children at the seder leave the table to open the door for Elijah, and upon their return, the cup is empty, signifying that Elijah has been in the home. Passover is the only holiday for which the Torah specifically states which foods may or may not be eaten. Most importantly, Jews are not permitted to eat *hamez* or leavened bread during any time over the Passover holiday. On the day before Passover, Jews must cleanse their homes of all traces of leavened bread. Several prayer services are held at the synagogue throughout Passover.

Yom Kippur or Day of Atonement is observed on the tenth day of Tishre (September-October) and represents a culmination of the Ten Days of Penitence which begin on Rosh Hashanah. It is the most solemn day in the Jewish year and is characterized by fasting and prayer. Whereas other holidays are often ignored by many secular Jews, Yom Kippur is typically observed even by those who would not describe themselves as religious. The laws concerning the observance of Yom Kippur are clearly outlined in the Jewish scriptures. According to the Bible, Jews are not permitted to work and must afflict their souls between the eve of the ninth and the eve of the tenth of Tishre. Specifically, five things are forbidden on Yom Kippur: eating and drinking, washing oneself for personal grooming, the wearing of leather shoes, anointing the body, and conjugal relations. The punishment for indulging in these pleasures is said to be destruction. Children, pregnant women, and the sick are generally exempted from observing the laws of Yom Kippur. Jews are expected to attend five prayer services on Yom Kippur. The first, which is held on the evening of the ninth of Tishre, is known as Kol Nidre and serves to mark the beginning of the holiday. Between the morning and the afternoon of the tenth of Tishre, three services are held. The final service, known as Neilat She'arim (Closing of the Gates) is characterized by the blowing of the shofar (a trumpet made from a ram's horn). While the exact purpose for sounding the shofar is unknown, it is generally believed to signify the joyous nature of the end of Yom Kippur.

The principal element which characterises prayer during the Day of Atonement is confession, which is made silently before God. Prayers, which ask for forgiveness and mercy, are also important components of the Yom Kippur services. As on other holidays, specific portions of the holy scriptures are read. During the morning service, Leviticus 16 is read. This is then followed by the reading of Isaiah 57:15-58 and Numbers 29:7-11 (*maftir*). In the afternoon, Leviticus 18 (Torah) and the book of Jonah and Micah 7:18-20 are recited.

There are many customs associated with Yom Kippur. Some people prepare for the festival by ritual cleansing. In recent years, it has been customary to bless one's children on the eve of the Day of Atonement. On the actual day, many light candles and say a blessing over them. A standard Jewish prayer called the Amidah and parts of the Shema, which are normally read silently, are read aloud. While it is not required, some individuals remain standing during all five prayer services.

Boys and girls are initiated into the Jewish religious community when they are eight days old.

In the case of a girl a special blessing is said and she is formally given her name by her father; normally this will happen in the presence of members of the wider family. In the case of a boy the ceremony is more involved. An act of circumcision is performed in obedience to the Torah where God instructs Abraham that 'every male among you [i.e. your family clan] shall be circumcised' (Genesis 17:11-12): circumcision is the removal of part or all of the foreskin which covers the glans of the penis. From this act the ceremony gets its name, *Brit Milah*, 'the covenant of cutting'. A specially trained individual called a Mohel performs circumcision, which may occur either at home or in a hospital. After the procedure is completed the Mohel will say a benediction over a glass of wine and then add a second benediction praising God. Relatives and friends pass on their good wishes to the child, expressing the hope that he will grow up to study the Torah and follow its instruction. The father may make a symbolic offering in the synagogue of five shekels as a sign of the child's dedication to God.

The next important life cycle event for a young Jewish boy or girl is the Bar Mitzvah or Bat Mitzvah respectively. A boy is

Bar Mitzvah when he reaches his thirteenth birthday, while a girl is Bat Mitzvah when she is twelve, though the ceremony may be postponed to her thirteenth birthday as well. The literal meaning of Bar/Bat Mitzvah is 'Son or Daughter of the Law'. Historically Bar Mitzvah or Bat Mitzvah is the ceremonial occasion that marks the time when a young person is recognised as an adult member of the Jewish community and is hereafter responsible for performing mitzvot, i.e. keeping the commandments. For example, before his Bar Mitzvah a young boy is not expected to fast on Yom Kippur but after Bar Mitzvah, he is required to fast. At Bar Mitzvah he is also counted in the minyan, a quorum of ten required to conduct a service (traditionally in Orthodox Judaism ten males are required). The Bar/Bat Mitzvah ceremony consists of the young person chanting the blessings, and reading a portion in Hebrew from the Torah. On this occasion it is customary for boys to be presented with a prayer shawl (*tallit*) and a prayer book (*siddur*). He may also receive a phylactery (*tephellin*) to wear – this is a small box containing passages from the Torah, worn on the forehead and arm during morning prayers. In preparation for the day of Bar/Bat Mitzvah Jewish children attend religious classes where they learn about Jewish customs, holidays, history, and the Hebrew language.

In the Torah, the origins of marriage are traced back to Adam and Eve, and according to one Jewish tradition, it is God who officiated at their marriage. Marriage is God's intention for human beings and sex should be sanctified by marriage. Moreover, one of the *mitzvot* (commandments) of the Torah is to be fruitful and multiply. In the time of the Hebrew Bible, marriages were arranged. While romantic love did exist, parents generally sought out appropriate partners for their children. This practice of arranging unions between men and women usually involved the services of a *shadchan* or matchmaker. In addition a man wishing to marry paid a sum of money (bride price) to the father for his daughter. A small sum is still paid in some communities to symbolise this earlier practice.

An Orthodox wedding cannot occur on certain days of the Jewish calendar. For example, one cannot get married on Shabbat or on days of fasting. Traditionally Jewish brides would wear white at their wedding to symbolise purity. The Shabbat before the wedding, the groom (and bride in liberal Judaism) is called up to read the blessings over the Torah. This ceremony is called the *aufruf*. A rabbi usually conducts the marriage ceremony though any prominent male member of the Orthodox community may officiate. Most weddings take place in the synagogue but there is no requirement for a synagogue to be used. Sometimes weddings are conducted outdoors or in a hotel. The couple and the Rabbi stand under the *huppah* or marriage canopy. A huppah can be a tallit shawl or a velvet cloth. Friends of the couple use four poles to support it. There are many other rituals that Jewish people perform depending on the school of Judaism to which they belong. For example, Orthodox Jews have the bride circle the man seven times during the ceremony to symbolise her courting of the groom. In an Orthodox ceremony the *Ketubah* or marriage contract is read aloud and signed. This agreement sets out how the husband will support his wife and how they will fulfil their spiritual and material responsibilities. The Ketubah serves to protect the rights of the bride and ensure her interests are protected. Following this blessings are spoken and Psalms 100 and 150 may be sung. Another well-observed custom is that of the groom breaking a glass at the end of the ceremony. This tradition is accorded different meanings. It is often said to remind Jews of the destruction of the Temple. The loud noise made by the breaking glass is also said to ward off any evil spirits. A celebration follows the ceremony where family and friends wish the couple a happy future and the blessing of children.

Traditionally there are a series of customs that a Jewish family and community perform as their loved one approaches death, and then for some time after the person passes on. When approaching death an observant Jew will confess his sins or recite the Shema. A member of the immediate family will also tend to remain in the room with the dying person. After death and the body is moved to the funeral home, someone from the funeral home accompanies it, reciting prayers until the appropriate time for burial. It is important in Jewish culture for the body to be buried as soon as possible. Before the family goes to the funeral chapel or synagogue for the service, the home where *shivah* (seven days of formalized mourning) is going to be observed is prepared. All the mirrors of the home are covered with either paper or a white scouring powder. There are two reasons for this custom. As death is a time of great sorrow, the bereaved are not to be concerned with their outer physical appearance. A second reason is that it was once believed that the spirit of the person who looked in the mirror could be snatched away by the deceased. Some undertakers will send people to the house to prepare the home, though some families cover the mirrors themselves. Just before going to the service one performs the ritual of cutting *keriah*, the tearing of a garment. The tears are not fully repaired, symbolising the never fully repaired loss of a loved one. A Rabbi and a Cantor usually conduct the funeral service. For the duration of the service the family may either sit in a private area or in the front row of the synagogue. After the traditional prayers are sung, the Rabbi will offer a eulogy. This is an opportunity to pay honour to the deceased.

The mourners then proceed to the cemetery for the burial. The time at the cemetery is very solemn. The casket is carried to the grave feet first so that the deceased's soul might not be tempted to look back. The casket is lowered into the ground as prayers are recited. Family and friends then symbolically fill the grave with dirt. At the conclusion of the burial, the loved ones return home. Before entering, they must remember to wash their hands. This custom originates from the belief that one needs to wash away the impurity that is part of death.

The observation of shivah will now begin and will end seven days later. Upon entering the home, a family member lights a shivah candle that acts as a sign of respect for the deceased. This candle will burn for the entire seven day period. Other family members and friends visit the shivah house and provide support. All sit on chairs that are very close to the ground. The reasoning behind this is that the chairs are uncomfortable, as is the time of mourning, and secondly, the shivah chairs enable one to be close to the ground, hence close to their loved one. Friends and family often send platters of food to the shivah house so that those who are in mourning need not be bothered with food preparation. The mourner's *Kaddish* (a prayer recited for the dead) is recited three times a day: morning, afternoon and in the evening during the seven days of shivah. Following the seven days of shivah the candle goes out, the mirrors are exposed and one can begin to mourn in a less formal way. For the next year a member of the congregation or another mourner says the Kaddish every day. Some time after the burial the headstone is unveiled in a ceremony with family and friends.

2.4   CHALLENGES TO THE TRADITION

The issue of identity has historically been central to Judaism. The Jews are a chosen people, set apart from others to receive God's revelation of the Torah and required to fulfil its statutes. The Jewish tradition traces its origins back to Abraham and Moses and the creation of a people dedicated to the service of God. Many Jews regard themselves as related biologically to the original founders of Judaism. Biological identity plays a role in Judaism that it does not play in other religions. A true Jew is one who is born of a Jewish mother. Interpreted strictly this entails that Judaism is not a missionary religion. One may convert to Judaism, but it is an arduous and difficult task that typically requires years of instruction. Judaism does not actively seek converts. Of course one contributory factor for this stance may well be that persistent persecution by Christians dulled any sense of mission that the Jews once entertained in Graeco-Roman times, when converts were welcomed and sought.

The tension within Judaism between biological identity and religious identity has an even more acute manifestation than that relating to the subject of conversion to Judaism. The sharpest point at which the tension emerges is that of the relationship of secular Jews to Judaism. What is the relationship of Judaism as a historical group claiming a common (ethnic) ancestry to that of Judaism as a religious community dedicated to the service of God? In liberal, and increasingly pluralist, Western democracies individuals have the freedom to choose to practise religion or not. In the modern post-Enlightenment world a significant number of Jews have availed themselves of this freedom and renounced the practice of formal religion. Sometimes they are referred to as 'secular' Jews. But in what sense are they Jews? Can one be a Jew while denying the existence of the God of Israel? There are Jews who observe the main festivals of Judaism, particularly Yom Kippur, who profess to be agnostic regarding the fundamental *religious* tenets of Judaism; and there are those who become members of liberal synagogues in countries like the United States who do so for social rather than religious reasons. To be a Jew is for them to identify with the Jewish community.

In an Irish context the issue of identity has come to dominate all others for the simple reason that the Jewish communities in Ireland, chiefly located in Belfast and Dublin, are becoming smaller. Increasing mobility in response to employment trends, educational opportunities elsewhere and the allure of returning to Israel have resulted in a decline in numbers. This means that the community is getting smaller and finding it more difficult to preserve its distinctive identity. Jewish parents want their children to marry Jews, but as the community declines in numbers so the pool of available Jewish partners get smaller and hence the temptation to marry outside one's own community becomes greater. In such marriages the connections to Judaism are necessarily weakened. Jews are assimilated into other communities and the Jewish population further declines. Fear of assimilation in turn encourages parents to move elsewhere to join larger and more vibrant Jewish communities in the hope of maintaining their distinctive traditions and values. The issue of identity is not unique to Judaism and it will resurface in our discussions of other religions, particularly in contexts where for historical reasons a religion has come to be closely identified with an ethnic group. There are two other related issues for contemporary Judaism that are important in their own right, even though they also relate to the question of Jewish identity. The legacy of the Holocaust raises questions at a number of different levels for Jews. For some radical Jewish theologians the Holocaust means that Jews should renounce their faith in God. In the face of the annihilation of over six million of their number during the Second World War, the question is posed how can Jews believe in a sovereign God who directs their historical pilgrimage? Not that the persecution of Jews is a modern phenomenon. The matter of Christian complicity in anti-Semitism down the years should make uncomfortable reading for Christians, with anti-Jewish sentiment, ideas and practices present at all levels of the Churches' hierarchy, personnel and institutions. For other Jews, a proper response to the Holocaust is to persevere in the traditions of Judaism, for only in such a way can the aim of anti-Semitism be thwarted. The aim of anti-Semitism is to destroy Jewish culture and religion; it is only if Jews preserve their religious heritage that anti-Semitism is defeated. According to Emil Fackenheim, to abandon Jewish culture and religion is for Jews to abet in their own extermination.

This line of reasoning has persuaded many Jews that the best hope of overcoming persecution is to actively support the state of Israel. Israel provides the context where Judaism can be faithfully practised, culturally and religiously, without fear of persecution and bigotry. But what kind of state should Israel become? Should it be a religious state where the traditions of Judaism are protected by legislation or should it aspire to be a liberal, pluralist democracy where equal rights are extended to all? There is also the issue of the Palestinians and those marginalised and displaced by the creation of Israel as a sovereign state. What attitude to the Palestinians is consistent with faithfulness to the God of the 'people of Israel?'

3

Christianity

God sent his only Son into the world so that we might
live through him. In this is love, not that we loved God
but that he loved us and sent his Son to be the atoning
sacrifice for our sins. Beloved, since God loved us so
much, we also ought to love one another.

(John 4:9-11)

Christianity takes its name from its founder, Jesus Christ. The
term 'Christ' or *'Christos'* in Greek was originally a title derived
from a Hebrew word meaning the 'anointed One', in the sense of
one chosen and commissioned by God for a special task. The
English title 'Messiah' is equivalent to the term Christ: the former
is derived from the Hebrew language and the latter is derived
through the Greek language of New Testament times. Jesus is the
Messiah, Israel's long promised deliverer and saviour – the name
Jesus means 'God saves'. Christianity is properly described as a
salvation religion, in that Christians believe that God became
incarnate in the person of Jesus Christ in order to save humankind
from sin and spiritual death. It is also a missionary religion, in that
everyone has disobeyed and deserves punishment, but God in
Christ has acted in history to redeem and to save those who are
penitent and who turn in faith to him.

An overview of Christianity

The Christian faith is directly descended from the religion of the Jews. Christians speak of the Hebrew Bible as the Old Testament and complement it with the New Testament, the collection of inspired writings that recount and explain the significance of Jesus Christ for Christians. Christianity's claimed continuity with the religion of the Jews up to the time of Jesus means that its beliefs and practices can be traced back historically to the teaching of the Old Testament. Jewish teaching about God, salvation, and God's covenant with Israel provides the foundation upon which Christianity has erected its own distinctive belief system.

God

Christians, like Jews and Muslims, believe in the existence of one God who created the universe and rules over it. There is a root concept of deity common to all three religions, however much they disagree on other things. God is omniscient, omnipotent, omnipresent and eternal. He is self-sufficient and transcendent: the world is not God or a part of God. He is the creator and all else in the universe of space and time is created by God. Furthermore, he is intimately involved with his creation. All three religions speak of God as gracious and merciful, though within and between the religions these features of the character of God are subject to different interpretations. At the heart of Christianity is the assertion that God is holy love. God is morally perfect in every way and he abhors wrongdoing and evil. Yet he also loves. It is because God is loving that Christians believe he became incarnate in the person of Christ. The Apostle Paul says that 'God was in Christ reconciling the world to himself.' By virtue of his life of obedience to God the Father and his sacrificial death on the cross, Christ has the power to redeem from slavery to sin all those who put their faith in him and become members of God's community, the Church, the visible body of Christ on earth. As the early Church reflected on the nature of God in the light of their experience of deliverance and renewal through Christ so they came to the conclusion that Jesus was both truly man and truly God. Further reflection on the implications of the New Testament witness to God convinced them that the Spirit was also God.

The life and teaching of Jesus

What distinguishes Christianity from other religions is the significance that it attaches to the person and work of Christ. Christians believe that God is as Christ has revealed him to be. It is not just that Jesus reveals God by his teaching and example; rather it is that Jesus is God in the flesh. Jesus is God incarnate. This truth is affirmed in the early Christian creeds – the Apostles' Creed and the Nicene Creed, for example. Such a belief also seems the natural extension of some of the designations of Jesus in the New Testament. The Apostle Paul speaks of Jesus as 'the image of the invisible God' (Colossians 1:15) and as in 'the form of God' (Philippians 1:6). John the Evangelist describes Jesus as the agent of creation who as the Word 'was with God, and … was God' (John 1:1). The early Jewish disciples, who were monotheists, worshipped Jesus and encouraged others to do likewise – worship is appropriate to God alone. It is from such insights and material that the later doctrine of the Trinity was forged.

The main events of Jesus' life are well known and are recounted, albeit from slightly different perspectives, in the four gospels. The story of his birth to a virgin, Mary, in a stable in Bethlehem is told in the Gospels of Matthew and Luke: biblical scholars have noted that the account of Jesus' birth in Matthew is written from Joseph's perspective, whereas the account in Luke is from Mary's perspective. Jesus' birth is believed by Christians to be the fulfilment of prophecies in the Jewish Old Testament that predicted that the Messiah would deliver the Jewish people from captivity and oppression. After the story of his birth, and a short account of a visit to Jerusalem as a boy, little is known about Jesus until he began his ministry at the age of about thirty. His request to be baptised by his cousin, John the Baptist, and his journey into the wilderness where he was tempted by the Devil, mark the beginning of his ministry. He then spent three years wandering about as a teacher, healer and miracle worker. He taught in parables – everyday stories that have a divine message for those who interpret them correctly. Most of his teaching focused on the kingdom of God. He proclaimed that God's kingly rule was about to break into history and a decision had to be made either to respond or to oppose God. Repentance from past sins and commitment to a new radical form of obedience to God were the requirements of a positive response to Jesus' message. Ironically, many of the religious leaders and many within the religious establishment opposed his teaching and his radical call for all to repent. Jesus claimed that he spoke and acted with the authority of God and it was inevitable that his teaching, which seems to challenge the traditions of the Pharisees and the political security enjoyed by the Sadducees, would eventually bring him into serious conflict with the authorities. During the feast of Passover, probably three years after he has begun his public ministry, he was betrayed by one of his disciples, Judas Iscariot (in fact one of the 'Twelve', the group to which he had entrusted a leadership role within the wider circle of his followers). After questioning by the Jewish Sanhedrin council he was handed over to the Romans as a revolutionary. He was unfairly tried, condemned and put to death by means of crucifixion, though only after some equivocation by Pilate, the Roman Governor.

According to the unanimous witness of his earliest disciples, however, his death was not the end. On the Sunday following his execution, some of his female disciples discovered that the tomb into which his body had been placed was empty. He was resurrected from the dead and 'alive for evermore'. Over the next number of weeks, Jesus appeared to his disciples on numerous occasions, teaching them about the significance of his life and ministry. In his last appearance to the Twelve, he instructed them to 'Go ... and make disciples of all nations, baptising them in the name of the Father and of the Son and of the Holy Spirit.' After this, according to the Gospel accounts, he was taken up into heaven (this event is called the Ascension).

Schools of Christianity

There are many different varieties of Christianity in the world and the history of Protestantism after the Reformation is one of increasing division, debate and controversy. Only in the twentieth century with the birth of the Ecumenical Movement was there a slow realisation by Protestants that their many divisions compromised aspects of their mission and witness. Recognition that the Churches should work to overcome their divisions is now recognised by Catholics as well; and since Vatican II the Catholic Church has engaged in ecumenical efforts to restore visible unity to the church of Christ. Despite the existence of numerous independent Churches, Christian fellowships and denominations, it is nevertheless possible to identify three main branches of Christianity: the Roman Catholic Church, the Eastern Orthodox Church and Protestantism.

The Roman Catholic Church

It is the largest of the Christian denominations, with approaching a billion members. It traces its origins back through the Middle Ages to the early Church and particularly to the role of Peter within the Apostolic Church. The Catholic Church claims that it can trace continuity with the apostles and Christ through apostolic succession, i.e. that there is a valid chain of ministry and ordination going back to the ministry of Jesus. Roman Catholics believe in the primacy and authority of the Bishop of Rome (the Pope), who is regarded as Christ's representative on earth and the successor of St Peter (one of Jesus' disciples and the first Bishop of Rome, hence *Roman*

Catholicism, though Catholicism is now commonly used as an abbreviation). When defining matters of faith or morals what the Pope says is regarded as infallible and binding on all Catholics. The Catholic Church accords a high authority to ancient tradition and to the developing nature of Christian belief and practice. Traditionally it has accorded a significant role in the Church to Mary, the Mother of Jesus, and to the Saints: they not only provide patterns of holiness for others to follow, but also may intercede on behalf of others. Both the Roman Catholic and Orthodox Churches recognise seven sacraments: baptism, confirmation, eucharist, marriage, ordination, penance (sacrament of reconciliation), and the anointing of the sick (once called extreme unction).

In recent history, the most important event within the Catholic Church has been the Second Vatican Council (1962–65), convened under the direction of Pope John XXIII. His vision for the Council was that it would enter into dialogue with modern thought in order to communicate the Gospel of Christ more effectively to the world. Important developments in the Church have occurred as a result of Vatican II. There is a new spirit of co-operation between the Catholic Church and other Christian Churches, and between the Catholic Church and adherents of other religions. A new mandate was given to the different national Catholic Churches to relate the Gospel to their own particular cultural situations and contexts. One result of this emphasis has been a growing concern with social justice and efforts to reduce the degree of poverty and injustice suffered by many in the world.

Orthodox or Eastern Churches
One of the most influential acts of Emperor Constantine was his decision in 330 to move the capital of the empire from Rome to 'New Rome,' the city of Byzantium, at the eastern end of the Mediterranean Sea. The new capital, Constantinople (now Istanbul), also became the intellectual and religious focus

of Eastern Christianity. While Western Christianity became increasingly centralised, with the Pope at the top of a hierarchical system, the principal centres of the East – Constantinople, Jerusalem, Antioch, and Alexandria – developed their own distinctive form of Christianity – a lack of a centralised authority, close ties to the empire, and the development of a mystical tradition of liturgy and contemplation. Veneration of icons goes back to this period and it remains an important part of public and private worship in Orthodox Churches. The split with the western Church came about because of conflict over the Pope's claim to supreme authority and a clause added to the Church's creed which said that the Holy Spirit 'proceedeth from the Father *and the Son'*. No doubt these religious differences were accentuated by political intrigue and rival claims to pre-eminence. Historians often trace the final schism or division to 1054, when the respective Bishops of Rome and Constantinople exchanged excommunications with each other.

The four ancient centres of Eastern Christianity remain to this day – Alexandria, Antioch, Jerusalem and Constantinople. Each centre has a patriarch who acts as a spiritual leader and director for each independent Orthodox Church. The Churches extend across Eastern Europe, Slav countries and the eastern Mediterranean. Monasteries have played an important part in the history of the Eastern Christianity and Mount Athos in Greece has been a monastic centre since the tenth century. Clergy may marry, though bishops are typically chosen from those who are unmarried. There are over 214 million Orthodox Christians today.

Protestant Churches
The Reformation, which marked the birth of Protestantism, may be seen as the convergence of a number of factors, such as the call for reform in the Church, the growth of nationalism, and the emergence of the 'spirit of capitalism.' Martin Luther

was the catalyst that precipitated the new movement. His personal struggle for certainty of God's forgiveness led him to question the medieval system of salvation and the authority of the Church. His excommunication by Pope Leo X proved to be an irreversible step toward the division of Western Christendom. The movement was not confined to Luther's Germany. Native reform movements in Switzerland found leadership in Ulrich Zwingli and especially in John Calvin, whose *Institutes of the Christian Religion* became the most influential summary of the new theology. The English Reformation, provoked by the troubles of King Henry VIII, reflected the influence of both Lutheran and Calvinist reforms, but went its own 'middle way,' retaining Catholic elements such as the historic episcopate alongside Protestant elements such as the sole authority of the Bible. More radical Reformation groups, notably the Anabaptists, set themselves against other Protestants as well as against Rome, rejecting such long-established practices as infant baptism and denouncing the alliance of Church and state. Such alliances, however, helped to determine the outcome of the Reformation, which succeeded where it gained the support of the new national states. Translations of the Bible into the vernacular helped to foster new forms of spirituality and to shape the language and literature of the people. It also gave fresh stimulus to biblical preaching and to worship in the vernacular, for which a new hymnody came into being. Because of its emphasis on the participation of all believers in worship and confession of the faith, the Reformation developed systems of instruction in doctrine and ethics, especially in the form of catechisms, and an ethic of service to the world.

Protestantism has traditionally defined itself over against Catholicism. Positively, it affirms the sufficiency of the teaching of the Christian Scriptures as providing all that is necessary for salvation and Christian living. Equally it affirms the priesthood of all believers. Negatively, it rejects the primacy and infallibility of the Pope; it denies that there are seven sacraments (accepting baptism and the Lord's Supper as the only two sacraments instituted by Christ); it denies the efficaciousness of prayers for the departed and of prayers to the Saints; and it denies the doctrine of transubstantiation. Emphasis is placed upon individual decision and a life of commitment.

In recent years there has been an increasing recognition by the Churches of the beliefs and values that they hold in common and of their collective responsibility as inheritors of orthodox Christianity. The historical divisions between the Churches now appear insignificant when compared with the Christian/secular division in society that reveals itself in educational debates, social issues and personal morality. Recognition of this has inspired some theologians (Thomas Oden is a good example) to call upon the Churches to collaborate more closely in the cause of defending and affirming orthodox Christianity. In this way old oppositions and conflicts maybe transcended as the Churches witness together in unity to a 'disbelieving' world.

3.1   A VISION OF SALVATION

Christians believe that salvation is a gift from God to be received by faith. In his Gospel, John the Evangelist affirms that 'God so loved the world that whosoever *believes in him* shall not perish but have everlasting life' (John 3:16). The initiative in salvation is with God, who in the person of his Son, Jesus Christ, entered history in order to redeem sinful humanity. The church is the community of the 'saved', those who are called by God and who have responded to his call.

The story of salvation begins for Christians in events that are recorded in the Old Testament, and take us back to the origin of the world and humanity's place in it. God created the universe and placed Adam and Eve in the Garden of Eden as rulers over creation who were responsible to God for their stewardship. The story of Adam's disobedience or Fall provides the essential context for Christian teaching about salvation. Adam's sin initiated a pattern of disobedience in others that continues to this day. The Apostle Paul says that 'All have sinned and fallen short of the glory of God', even though he also taught that human beings are created in the image and likeness of God. According to St Augustine the image of God in men and women witnesses to the fact that humankind was created for fellowship with God and that life's true purpose and meaning is found only in communion with God: as he says 'our hearts are restless till they rest in thee'. Karl Barth has spoken of human disobedience as 'man's journey into the far country' by which he means that life without God is a journey away from our rightful human inheritance: it is a journey that brings alienation from God, from our neighbour and from ourselves. The individual is separated from the true source of life and away from what is right and good.

The Old Testament recounts the story of God's grace towards humankind and his decision to enter into a covenant with Abraham and his descendents. God promised Abraham that he would become the father of a great nation and that through him all the nations of the world would be blessed (a theme that the Apostle Paul explores in his Epistle to the Romans when he contends with his Jewish interlocutor that Abraham was justified by grace and not by works of the law). God's covenant with Abraham was subsequently reaffirmed to Moses. God was to save and redeem his people, i.e. the people of Israel, and they in turn were to obey his commandments and his law (Torah). All of life was regulated by the law – personal relationships, the preparation of food and the types of food appropriate for consumption (kosher), forms of worship and sacrifice, and so on. Israel's fortunes alternated, according to the prophets, on the basis of the nation's obedience to God: obedience brought blessing and disobedience brought judgement. By the first century of the Common Era Israel was ruled by the Romans, a sign to some that God's glory had departed and a sign to others that God's promised deliverance was at hand.

The narrative accounts of Jesus' life and ministry in the four Gospels present him as the fulfilment of Old Testament prophecies: the day of God's deliverance had arrived. Jesus died on the cross 'as a ransom for many' and to inaugurate God's rule in the world. The decisive battle against sin and the Devil has been won by virtue of Christ's sacrificial death and resurrection; history is now ushering towards its end and the final glorification of Christ as Lord and God over all. Christians live between the times, between the time of the victory of Christ and the time when his rule will be visible to all and God will be 'all in all'.

The Christian Church is entrusted with the good news that salvation is for all who repent and believe. There is no notion of salvation in the New Testament that does not entail membership of the community of God. The Church is the 'arc of salvation'. The Gospel of the Church brings freedom from sin and freedom for authentic existence. Christian freedom is of course a paradox; for it is only in service to God that true human freedom is realised. The freedom to serve oneself is, ironically, on a Christian understanding, to be a slave to sin. The church provides the context for the believer's daily struggle with sin as it ministers to those who strive to claim their inheritance as the 'sons of God'. This earthly pilgrimage may be one of endurance and effort, but by virtue of the Spirit's work in the believer it is one that leads upward to glory. The creeds of the Church speak of the confident hope of glory in the language of resurrection, a new life of participation in the glory of the resurrected Christ and in the company of the saints in heaven.

Salvation in Christianity includes past, present and future elements. Christ died to effect salvation for sinful humanity; the follower of Christ receives the benefits of Christ through the ministry of the Church in proclaiming the Gospel of Christ; and the Spirit in the believer is the guarantor that the salvation begun in hope ends in victory and final solicitude in heaven.

3.2   THE COMMUNITY OF BELIEVERS

The notion of community is central to Christianity, and is reinforced by the designation of the Church in the New Testament as 'the people of God' and by the Apostle Paul's description of the Church as 'the body of Christ' (Ephesians 1:22, Colossians 1:18 and 24). There are no solitary Christians in the New Testament. To become a follower or disciple of Jesus Christ was simultaneously to become a member of a community that was active in Christ's service. The modern notion of nominal Christianity is absent from the pages of the New Testament. Equally, the notion of a Christian who occasionally congregates with other Christians is absent. All Christians are assumed to be active in the local Christian community; and Paul expressly teaches that all Christians have a role to play (in the sense of a gift to exercise) within the local Christian community. This is the import of his teaching in Romans and in 1 Corinthians about the Gifts of the Spirit being distributed to individuals within the Church for 'the common good' and for 'building up' the congregation. The community of the Church is also the community of the Spirit, for those who are Church members are indwelt by the Spirit. It is the Spirit who leads to Christ and it is the Spirit who inspires the Church's worship and service to humanity. The community of the Church has also an important role to play in evangelism, for it is when there is unity and harmony within the community that those who are not members are challenged by the Gospel – they see a community that practises compassion and this acts as a witness to the truth of Christianity.

The notion of authority in the early Church is a disparate and wide-ranging category. The earliest Christians looked to the Hebrew Bible and interpreted the significance of Jesus in terms of its vocabulary and content. There was also the authority of experience. Christians could speak with authority of their experience of God, of changed lives and renewed relationships. In addition, the original disciples could speak of their experience of knowing Jesus and witnessing the events of his ministry. They received his teaching and they observed his healings and exorcisms. Their stories and recollections were passed on by word of mouth and used for a variety of purposes – to encourage, to instruct, to provide material for reflection and worship, and so on; it is largely from such sources that the Gospels were written. There were also more formal conferences, such as the Council of Jerusalem, where leaders in the Church came together to resolve disputes and regulate beliefs and practices. There was much debate over the conditions of entry of Gentiles into the Christian Church and this, on occasions, gave rise to bitter disputes, even among the apostles and leaders of the Churches. There was no single authority in the Church, perhaps except the authority of God in Christ, which of course was revealed in different ways – through Jesus' example and teaching, through prayer, through leaders in the church, through reflection upon Christian teaching, and so on. As time passed the notion of authority in the Church became more structured and formalised. As we have already noted, collections of stories about Jesus were edited to form the Gospels and the writings of celebrated Church apostles and leaders such as Paul, Peter and James were appended to the Gospels and exchanged between Churches. In this piecemeal fashion the documents of the New Testament were brought together. Alongside this development went the development of a more structured approach to ministry within the Church. Original charismatic leadership gave way by the second century to a threefold pattern of ministry comprising deacons, elders and bishops. In time, as the Church became predominantly Gentile (in that there were fewer Jewish followers of Jesus) and began to engage more closely with Gentile and predominantly Roman modes of thought so the term 'priest' replaced that of elder/presbyter as the designation of the local Christian leader of the community. Subsequent political and religious developments led to the emergence of the Bishop of Rome as the titular head of the Church of Christ on earth. At this point it becomes appropriate to speak of the Roman Catholic Church. But rather than confine ourselves to historical developments, we will instead turn to contemporary understandings of authority in the Church. Our focus will fall chiefly on the Roman Catholic Church because it is the Church to which the majority of Christians belong, though some reference will be made to the nature of authority within the Protestant Churches.

The Roman Catholic Church is a union of local churches (or dioceses) linked to each other by virtue of the fact that the bishop is in communion with the Bishop of Rome. The priest in each particular parish within the diocese is appointed by and represents the bishop. It is the role of the bishop to be the focal point of unity within each diocese and it is the role of the Bishop of Rome to be the focus of unity for the world-wide Church. Church authorities in Rome alone have the authority to move bishops from one diocese to another or to appoint priests to vacant bishoprics. The Roman Church has traditionally been hierarchical and centralised, though since Vatican II the practice of regional and national conferences of bishops meeting to discuss local issues and problems has encouraged the development of localised Catholic identities. The formation of parish councils with representatives from the community and more involvement by the laity in services, again both post-Vatican II developments, have also gone some way to moderating the hierarchical and centralised nature of traditional Catholicism.

The primacy of the Pope, together with his infallibility, became official dogmas of the church at the First Vatican

Council of 1870. These doctrines, though carefully defined by the Council, were interpreted in a somewhat autocratic way by a number of subsequent popes. Vatican II reasserted the primacy and infallibility of the Pope in matters of faith and doctrine, though the exercise of both are securely placed within the context of the responsibility of all the bishops of the Church to provide spiritual direction – this is referred to as the concept of collegiality. On this understanding the Pope speaks infallibly for the Church when he speaks on behalf of and with the support of the bishops.

Authority is accorded within Catholicism to the Scriptures as they have been interpreted within the Church and the Christian community. This authority is mediated by those who are entrusted by the Church to be guardians and interpreters of tradition. At the heart of Catholicism is the idea of an evolving and developing community of faith whose grasp of the truth becomes firmer and surer with time. Moreover, truth is important and for this reason those who present it are under the discipline of the Church. On this understanding any fully fledged notion of democracy in the Church is ill-advised and ill-conceived. God commands through the teaching organ of the Church and men and women are called to obedience.

The difference between the Protestant Churches' and the Catholic Church's attitude to authority, at a formal level at least, is easy to characterise. The former looks exclusively to the Christian Scriptures as containing all that is necessary to salvation, whereas the latter interprets Scripture within an ongoing, developing tradition that uncovers and reveals new insights and truths. Authority for the Protestant lies in what the Scriptures teach. If justification by grace through faith is taught; if Christ died as a satisfaction for sin; if sexual relations are to be confined to marriage; if there are only two sacraments instituted by Christ; if believers' baptism was practised in New Testament churches: if these doctrines are Scriptural then they should be believed. 'What do the Scriptures teach?' is the question that is central to Protestantism. Development and progress in the Church do not result from the recognition of new dogmas, but in the more faithful application to life of those beliefs essential to Biblical Christianity. Alongside the appeal to the Christian Scriptures, the authority of which the Church acknowledges rather than determines, is a certain disregard for institutional hierarchy and organisational structure. One of the defining features of Protestantism is its affirmation of the 'priesthood of all believers'. There are no special calling or levels of ministry. There is no priestly hierarchy or centralised teaching office that determines Christian faith and practice. The need for individual decision is paramount within Protestantism. Each individual must decide for himself or herself to follow Christ; there should be no unreflective membership of the Christian community. This individualistic spirit also extends to the content of belief, for each must decide what the Scriptures teach. Each must be convinced that what is believed and practised is in keeping with the teaching and example of the early Church as described in the Christian Scriptures. Some refer to this as the 'priority of private judgement'. Historically such a principle has yielded mixed results – deep and faithful commitment to the Church, alongside dissension and division. Yet it is easy to exaggerate the divisiveness of Protestantism. First, it is probably true to say that divisions have usually occurred over beliefs and practices that are not regarded by Protestants as central to the Gospel. In other words, Protestants are agreed (as are Catholics) in their assertion of the deity of Christ, the efficacy of his death as a sacrifice for sin, the necessity of repentance and faith in Christ, the need for a life of holiness and moral purity, and so on. Dissension and division has tended to focus on matters of Church order, ministry and discipline – over the appropriateness of episcopacy, whether infants are fit subjects for baptism and whether the monarch should be the symbolic head of a national church. Secondly, Protestants are not greatly concerned with uniformity and outward unity. They point to the looseness and diversity of

Church authority in New Testament times. What is important is that individuals respond to the Gospel of Christ and endeavour to live by it in different and changing circumstances. Agreement on the essentials is consistent with latitude on the non-essentials.

3.3   A CELEBRATING TRADITION

Important events in life are marked in different ways by religious people: birth, the transition to adulthood, marriage and death are all endowed with religious significance and acknowledged by ceremonies, some simple and some complex. The Catholic Church, the Eastern Orthodox Church and most branches of Protestantism receive infants into membership of the Church through the sacrament of baptism. Some Protestant denominations, such as the Baptists believe that baptism should be administered only to those who make a profession of faith in Christ. Consequently infants are not baptised, though there is normally an act of dedicating the child to God. While it is accepted that baptism confers Church membership there are important differences between Catholics and Protestants on the theology of baptism. Catholics believe that baptism cleanses from original sin, whereas Protestants regard baptism as an outward symbol of the need for the infant to grow up to renounce sin and turn to Christ.

In the early centuries of the Church confirmation typically followed immediately after baptism. This is because most of those who joined the Church were converts who responded as adults to the preaching of the Gospel. The rites of baptism, confirmation and Eucharist were celebrated on the same occasion. But as time went on more and more people were added to the Church as infants and not as believing adults. Accordingly, baptism and confirmation became separate church rituals. Confirmation became the occasion when individuals affirmed for themselves the promises made on their behalf by their parents at baptism. The Catholic Church teaches that confirmation is a ratification of the gifts of grace already received at baptism. The laying on of hands by the Bishop symbolises the gift of the Spirit that equips for service within the Christian community. It symbolises that the Christian life is to be lived in the grace that God imparts and not in the strength of one's own natural powers.

Marriage is regarded as a sacrament by the Catholic Church; it is not so regarded by the Protestant Churches. Whatever theological differences there are over marriage, the marriage ceremony is broadly similar in all Christian Churches. The marriage service may begin with an appropriate hymn and the priest or minister reminds the congregation of the meaning of marriage. The bride and groom make promises to each other, to love, cherish, and honour; traditionally the groom also promises to provide for his wife and the bride promises obedience. The priest or minister blesses the ring and this is placed on the third finger of the bride's left hand (a ring may also be worn by the groom), as the words, 'With this ring I thee wed' are said. The priest then pronounces them husband and wife and says: 'Whom God has joined together let no man put asunder'. Prayers are said and there are readings from the Bible and a homily/sermon. In a Catholic marriage service, the ceremony will be followed by a celebration of Mass.

The funeral rites of Christianity are fairly straightforward. People typically assemble in the church to remember the deceased and to express community support to the family of the deceased. Prayers are said, hymns are sung, and the deceased's life and achievements are recounted. In the Catholic funeral service Mass is celebrated for the deceased. The focus of the service is the promise of salvation and life after death in the company of Christ for those who believe in him. Burial may be in a grave or by cremation. The priest or minister speaks the word of committal and commends the person to God.

The Christian year

Christians of all traditions place a strong emphasis both on private devotion and on communal worship. Since New Testament times, the chief day for public worship is Sunday, the first day of the week, in commemoration of the resurrection of Christ. It is the time when Christians gather to hear the reading and preaching of the word of God in the Bible, to participate in the sacraments, and to pray, praise, and give thanks.

The Church year is divided into festivals and seasons. Some, like Christmas Day, happen on the same date every year, while others move around within a range of dates. The main festival that moves is Easter, and since many other festivals have their dates fixed in relation to Easter, they move with it.

The diagram of the Church Year shows the principal festivals and seasons.

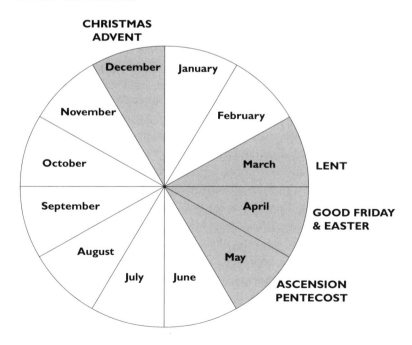

The season of Advent ('coming') is a preparation for Christmas and has been observed in the West from the time of Pope Gregory the Great (died 604 CE). The Christian year begins with the First Sunday in Advent, which occurs on the fourth Sunday before Christmas. In many churches an Advent candle is lit. On each of the following Sundays until Christmas another candle is lit, as a symbol to light the way to the child Jesus. In church services during Advent hymns are sung and portions of the Bible are read that look forward to the coming of the Messiah, whose birth is celebrated at Christmas. There is also a focus upon the anticipated future return of Christ as Lord over all creation and the need to be prepared to meet with him.

The pre-Christian Roman festival honouring the sun fell on 25th December but as more and more Romans embraced Christianity so this date came to be celebrated as the date of the birth of Christ. Christians celebrate Christmas by decorating the church with symbols of the story of the birth of Jesus – the crib and the holy family, the star and the angels, the shepherds and the wise men. Special services are held on Christmas Eve and on Christmas day. Christmas carols are sung to celebrate the birth of Jesus and its meaning in the context of 'salvation history'.

Lent is a very old name for the lengthening of the days of spring after winter. In the Christian calendar it is a time of penance and many Christians 'give something up for Lent'. Purple is the symbolic colour used in some churches throughout Lent, for drapes and altar frontals. Purple is used for two reasons: first, purple is associated with mourning and so anticipates the pain and suffering of the crucifixion; second, purple is the colour associated with royalty, and celebrates Christ's resurrection and sovereignty. The season of Lent begins on Ash Wednesday and continues for forty days and six Sundays before Easter day. (The Orthodox Churches do not observe Ash Wednesday.) Shrove Tuesday is the Tuesday before

Ash Wednesday and the beginning of Lent. It is a day of penitence – to cleanse the soul before Lent – and a day of celebration as the last chance to feast before Lent begins. Shrove Tuesday gets its name from the ritual of 'shriving' that Christians underwent in the past. In shriving (an old Anglo-Saxon word) a person confesses his sins and receives absolution for them. Ash Wednesday is so called because of the old custom of placing a piece of ash on the forehead in the form of a cross and wearing sackcloth as a sign of penitence. The symbol of the cross reminds the penitent of baptism. Interestingly, the ash is sometimes mixed with anointing oil in order to make a clear mark, and the use of such oil acts as a further reminder of the anointing with oil that takes place at baptism. The modern practice in Roman Catholic churches, as the ashes are being administered, is for the priest to say a word of challenge and invitation, such as 'Turn away from sin and believe the Gospel'. In some churches the worshippers leave with the mark still on their forehead so that they carry the sign of the cross out into the world. In other churches the service ends with the ashes being washed off as a sign that the participants have been cleansed of their sins.

Christians call the seven days before Easter Holy Week, when they follow the progress of Jesus during his last final in Jerusalem, from his entry into the city until his burial. They regard the events of these days as the most significant in Christianity.

Palm Sunday (also called Passion Sunday) is the Sunday before Easter. It is linked to the story of Jesus' triumphant entry into Jerusalem on his way to Crucifixion and death. In many Churches, during Palm Sunday services, large palm branches are carried in processions. In Roman Catholic and some Anglican Churches members of the congregation hold small crosses made of palm leaves, both to remember the palm leaves which the people of Jerusalem waved when Jesus arrived, and to remember the cross on which he died. Some Christians display the crosses from the service in their homes during the year as a symbol of their faith. Hymns for Palm Sunday usually include 'Ride on, Ride on in Majesty', and 'All glory, laud and honour'.

Maundy Thursday is the Thursday before Easter. Maundy comes from the Latin word for 'commandment': at the Last Supper Christ commanded his disciples to love one another. Christians remember it as the day when Jesus washed the feet of his disciples and inaugurated the Eucharist. In many other countries this day is known as Holy Thursday. The Roman Catholic Church's celebration of Maundy Thursday includes a ceremony in which the priest washes the feet of twelve people to commemorate Jesus' washing the feet of his disciples. It was common in monasteries throughout history for the Abbot to wash the feet of the monks in a similar gesture. Maundy Thursday is also the day on which the supply of anointing oil to be used in ceremonies during the year is 'consecrated'. This is done at a special 'Chrism Mass'.

Good Friday is the Friday before Easter and commemorates the execution of Jesus by Crucifixion. His body was taken down from the cross, and buried. The tomb was guarded and an enormous stone was put over the entrance, so that nobody could steal the body. Good Friday is the most solemn day of the Christian year, and is marked by special services and meditations. It is a day of mourning in church. Christians meditate on Jesus' suffering and death on the cross, and what this means for their faith. In some countries, there are special Good Friday processions, or re-enactments of the Crucifixion. The main service on Good Friday takes place between noon and 3pm. In many Churches it takes the form of a meditation based on the seven last words of Jesus on the cross, with hymns, prayers, and a short sermon.

Easter Day is the most important festival of the year for Christians, and perhaps the most joyous. (The name Easter is a form of an Anglo-Saxon word, *Eostre*, for the goddess of

Spring.) It celebrates the return of Christ from death after the Crucifixion. His followers realised that God had raised Jesus from the dead. Many Churches will mark Easter with a midnight vigil on the Saturday night. The church is sometimes decorated with Spring flowers for the services on Easter day. In the Catholic Church a paschal candle is lit and carried into the darkened church to symbolise the light of Christ's resurrection. The worshippers light their candles from this until the whole church is a blaze of light. The Easter paschal candle may be marked with the wounds of Christ and the first and last letters of the Greek alphabet (*Alpha* and *Omega*). The priests wear their brightest vestments. The reading tells the story of the resurrection and the sermon is typically on the theme of 'new life' in Christ. Worshippers may repeat the ancient response: 'The Lord is risen. He is risen indeed!'

The feast of Pentecost is the seventh Sunday after Easter (and ten days after the Feast of the Ascension of Christ to heaven). It celebrates the descent of the Holy Spirit onto the disciples, and is regarded as the birthday of the Christian Church. It is a particularly joyful festival in the charismatic Churches that celebrate the Spirit as the giver of 'gifts' for ministry and the building up of the community. Pentecost was also known as Whitsun (from the white robes worn by converts at their baptism). Where the clergy wear vestments the colour is red, to symbolise the flames of fire in which the Holy Spirit descended upon the disciples in the Upper Room.

3.4   CHALLENGES TO THE TRADITION

For the Gospel to be credible it has to relate to the diverse nations and peoples of the world. Christianity has to be relevant to people in different cultural situations. Theologians refer to this process of relating the Gospel to local cultures as 'inculturation'. As a result of Christianity's world mission and its efforts to be relevant to all humankind it is difficult to speak generally of challenges that apply to Christians everywhere. The challenges to Christianity in South Africa may be quite different from those encountered in the Philippines, which in turn may be quite different from those encountered in the United States of America or in Ireland. There is a need for Christian credibility in these different contexts, but the exact issue to which the Church needs to respond will vary from locality to locality and from nation to nation. The challenge of relevance is exacerbated for Christians by the fact that the Gospel does not provide a blueprint for all of life. There is no specifically Christian economic policy, no specifically Christian view on the level of provision of social rights, and so on. There may well be Christian principles that apply to these different issues but there is no straightforward set of Christian prescriptions that makes reflection unnecessary and excludes the possibility of others reaching different conclusions by reference to the same Christian principles. Unlike traditional Islam with its requirement that Islamic law (Sharia) be applied in the public sphere, the Christian mandate for society does not prescribe any particular set of laws and statutes that should be publicly affirmed and enforced. The notion of a Christian society remains coherent, but it is not now (as it once was) interpreted to mean that Christian beliefs and practices should be enforced by the civil and legal authorities on all citizens.

As a general statement the Church is credible to the degree to which it lives out the Gospel. When the Church equivocates on the truth and compromises on righteousness and justices, it loses credibility in the eyes of the world. If the Church is seen to place its own influence and social standing before the cause of social justice and the needs of the poor then it loses the trust of the people. The purpose of ministry is to serve and the Church is called to be a servant Church. As a rule, large organisations and institutions tend to develop bureaucracies that seek to perpetuate their own influence, and many Churches, unfortunately, have not been exceptions to this: the

Churches have also spawned large bureaucracies that seem unresponsive to the needs of the people. Maintaining the social influence of the organisation becomes more important than serving the Church and the world. It is embarrassing to report the instances in history when the Churches have aligned themselves with the rich and the powerful over against the poor, or when they have actively engaged in persecution of those with whom the Churches disagree, or simply remained silent before the oppression of those outside their particular congregations because they feared the loss of privilege and social influence. In one sense the greatest challenge to the Churches is to be faithful to the message that they have received from God. The practice of holiness and righteousness by the Churches is essential if they are to convince the world that the Gospel is true and that the church of Christ anticipates life in the kingdom of God.

In relating to the world the Church has to distinguish between that to which it has to relate positively and that to which it must react negatively. The Churches face challenges at different levels and from different sources. For example, how far can the Churches endorse gay rights and equal rights for women? Should the Church bless homosexual unions? Should the Catholic Church rethink its exclusion of women from the priesthood? There is also the issue of whether priests in the Catholic Church should be allowed to marry. In order to respond to such issues the Churches have to know their own mind and seek to be faithful to their own beliefs and values. The Apostle Paul warns against the danger of the 'the world pressing you [the Church] into its mould'. The Churches must respond to public interests and issues but they must do so in a way that does not compromise Christian truth and holiness. Some will regard the matters of gender equality and sexuality as aspects of a much greater challenge to the Churches – the challenge of social justice. What are the Churches doing to improve the lot of the poor and the oppressed in the world?

Have the Churches concerned themselves too much with the spiritual needs and welfare of individuals to the neglect of publicly challenging oppressive social and political structures that demean human dignity?

One other issue that is of particular relevance to contemporary Christianity is that of religious pluralism. Should there be greater co-operation between the different Churches and should they mutually recognise each other as equally valid expressions of authentic Christianity? There is also the issue of what some theologians have called 'the wider ecumenism', that is, the relationship between Christianity and the other great religions of the world. Is salvation confined to the Christian Churches or do other religions mediate God's grace and favour? Some see a positive interpretation of other religions as necessary to the cause of peace and harmony in the world whereas others enjoin respect for adherents of other religions alongside a traditional commitment to the exclusive truth of Christianity. Moreover, the belief that Christianity is true to a degree denied to other religions need not entail that all adherents of other religions, however noble and sincere, are excluded from God's salvation in Christ. The challenge of pluralism is to frame a response that is faithful to the nature and character of God as he has revealed himself to be in Christ.

4

Islam

There is no God but Allah, and Muhammad is his Prophet.

The Qur'an

Islam is the name given to the religion founded by Muhammad in Arabia in the early seventh century of the Common Era. The word 'Islam' is derived from the verb '*slm*', which means 'to resign, submit or surrender oneself', and *Islam* means the act of submission and resignation (to Allah – God). A Muslim is someone who professes Islam, someone who has submitted to Allah.

Islam is the second largest world religion, claiming over 800 million adherents. The majority of Muslims live in North Africa, in countries such as Algeria, Libya and Egypt, and throughout the Middle East, in Saudi Arabia, Iran and Iraq. There are over forty countries where Islam is the dominant religion, and there are also significant Muslim populations in such diverse political and geographical environments as the Soviet Union, China, India, England and the USA.

Islam belongs to the monotheistic family of religions that includes Judaism and Christianity. Like them it is a prophetic religion. According to the Qur'an, the Muslim holy book, Islam was the religion of all the prophets from Adam to Muhammad. This venerable line of prophets includes Abraham, Moses, Elisha, Jonah and Jesus. Muhammad, however, is the seal of the prophets: the last and the greatest. To him was entrusted the Qur'an, God's final, definitive word to humankind, in the light of which all other revelations have to be corrected and extended.

An overview of Islam

The religion of Islam centres upon Allah's revelation of himself and his message in the Qur'an. Allah is a God of action and initiative and throughout history he has revealed his message to special individuals. From the origin of the world, Allah sought to direct men and women towards their destiny as servants of Allah, in whose service is found perfect peace and solicitude. Special individuals were chosen to carry God's message to their families, clans and nations. The last and greatest of the prophets was Muhammad, to whom God dictated the words of the Qur'an. Whereas other prophets received Allah's words and passed them on in their own distinctive ways (and on occasions incorporating error), with Muhammad Allah's words were received and directly committed to memory. When Muhammad spoke in Allah's name, he repeated the message that Allah had given him, without gloss or emendation. The authority of the Qur'an is inextricably linked to the authority of Muhammad, and for this reason it is important to look briefly at Muhammad's life and ministry.

Muhammad

Muhammad was born around 570 CE into a relatively wealthy Meccan family (Mecca continues as a city to this day within the modern state of Saudi Arabia). His father, Abdullah, died before he was born and his mother, Aminah, died when he was six years old. He was brought up, first by his grandfather, and upon his grandfather's death by his uncle, Abu Talib. Earliest records portray Muhammad as a sensitive and religious youth. He is said to have distanced himself from the polytheism and animism of his immediate religious environment. It is also more than likely that in caravan travels with his uncle, who was a merchant, he encountered different forms of Christianity, many of them unorthodox and heretical.

His interest in religion continued into adult life. Even when married, for he had married a wealthy widow, Kadijah, fifteen years his senior in 595 CE, he continued his practice of retiring to Mount Hira, a mountain near Mecca, for prayer and reflection. It was on one such 'retreat', Muslims believe, at the age of forty that he was called to be a 'messenger of God' (*rasul Allah*, this is the most common title used of Muhammad in the Qur'an). This event is recorded in the Qur'an:

> In the name of God, the Compassionate, the Merciful
> Recite in the name of your Lord who created,
> Created man from clots of blood!
> Recite! Your Lord is the most Bountiful One,
> Who by the pen taught man what he did not know.
>
> (Surah 96)

On returning home, Muhammad was encouraged in his calling to be a spokesperson for Allah by his faithful wife. He embarked on his mission by challenging the immorality of the inhabitants of Mecca. He focused on God's word of judgement against idolatry and polytheism. He preached that God was angry at human pride and self-centredness, which expressed itself in the worship of idols and the gods of nature. With prophetic faithfulness and fervour he railed against all forms of ungodliness, warning his hearers that there was a judgement after death in which Allah would reward the righteous and punish the unrighteous. His first followers came from his own family, his wife Khadijah, Abu Talib, and Zaid, an adopted son who had formerly been his slave, a gift to him from Khadijah.

The first adult outside the family to make profession of Islam was Abu Bakr, a fellow wealthy merchant. Other converts followed, but numbers remained small. Most of the inhabitants of Mecca rejected Muhammad's message and many were enraged by his implacable opposition to the worship of crafted images of the gods (for Mecca was a pilgrimage centre and many of its inhabitants benefited both from the manufacture and sale of such images). For a time Muhammad was protected by his clan, the Quarish, who were influential and powerful, but finally it became clear to him that Mecca was no longer safe for him and his fledgling religious community. In 622 CE he took advantage of an invitation from some tribesmen from Yathrib (later renamed Medina) who were sympathetic to his teaching and who were eager to find a new leader to adjudicate between different parties and factions within the city. This flight or Hijra was the turning point of Muhammad's career, and was later chosen to mark the beginning of the Muslim era and calendar.

The different tribes and factions in Yathrib united under Muhammad's leadership. At the beginning even the Jews and the Christians welcomed him, no doubt encouraged by his uncompromising monotheism and his criticism of idolatry. Later events in the city alienated both groups, but by the time this occurred Muhammad's authority was well established. The daily pattern of religious life as followed by Muslims today can be traced back to this period of Muhammad's ministry, as he forged a new religious community, charged with carrying out Allah's commands to the letter. Much that is recorded in the Qur'an comes from this period. Community life was consolidated in common practices and commitments. The new faith with its emphasis on a religious allegiance that transcended clan and tribal loyalties attracted more and more followers. The community (the Umma) prospered under Muhammad's firm and uncompromising leadership. Moreover, Muhammad revealed himself to be a talented military tactician as well as a gifted community leader. In a succession of battles against the Meccans

(Badr 624, Uhud 625, and Ahzad 627) he impressed his followers with his tenacity and bravery. Eventually by persistence and effort he wore down Meccan opposition and by 629 CE he and his followers were able to enter the city of Mecca victoriously. His first act was to clear the Kaaba shrine of its numerous statues of the gods and to rededicate it to the worship of Allah the true and living God. According to Muhammad the original site of the Kaaba, which contains a black meteorite stone, was the place where the prophet Abraham had shown his faithfulness to God by his readiness to sacrifice his son, Ishmael (this story contrasts with the Jewish story, where it is Isaac who is offered in sacrifice). In this new form the Kaaba would continue as a place of pilgrimage.

Muhammad made Mecca his home and from there directed his armies in the expansion of Islam. Alas his enjoyment of success and acclaim was short lived, for in 632 CE, only three years after claiming Mecca for Islam, he died. According to tradition, his death was announced to his followers with these words:

> Let him know, who worshipped Muhammad, that Muhammad is dead;
> but whosoever worships God, let him know that God lives and never dies.

Muhammad was a messenger of God, the last and the greatest of God's messengers. Although regarded by many Muslims as perfect in every way, he is nevertheless regarded as human and not divine.

The Qur'an

According to Muslim tradition, Muhammad could neither read nor write. Muslims regard his lack of literary talent as underlining the miraculous nature of the Qur'an: the beauty of its language witnesses to the conclusion that it is not a human work, but a revelation from God. Throughout Muhammad's ministry he received messages from God, and it is the content of these messages that collectively make up the Qur'an. During his lifetime the process of collecting these messages was initiated by his followers, but it was only after his death that serious attempts were made to bring together and order all of the revelations Muhammad had received. Within twenty years a final definitive edition of the Qur'an was produced, under the direction of the third official successor (Calaphite) to Muhammad.

The word 'recite' (*iqra*) is the word from which Qur'an is derived. The Qur'an is a recitation, or thing to be recited. As a religious text it should be read and recited in the original Arabic language, for this is the language in which the revelation was originally given by God. For this reason Muslim children, whatever their first language, are encouraged to learn Arabic or at least encouraged to learn to recite portions of the Qur'an in Arabic. To read God's actual words, even without understanding, is efficacious and bestows a blessing on the reader. In some cases devout Muslims memorise the entire contents of the Qur'an: the title '*hafiz*' is given to such a person.

A copy of the Qur'an, in the form of a 'guarded tablet', is kept in the presence of Allah (Qur'an 85:12). It is about the same length as the Christian New Testament and has 114 chapters or *surahs* of unequal length. In Oriental editions the surahs are not numbered and simply carried the chapter heading given in the original collection made by Uthman. Broadly, the surahs are arranged in order of length, going from the longest to the shortest. Each surah, except the ninth, entitled 'Repentance', begins with the phrase 'In the Name of Allah, the Compassionate, the Merciful'.

The teachings of the Qur'an
Traditionally there are five articles of faith to which Muslims subscribe.

God

The unanimous teaching of the revelations collected in the Qur'an is that God is one. 'There is no God but Allah!', this is the first line of the *Kalima*, the creed that is recited five times daily by Muslims. There is only one God; he is absolute and real, omniscient and omnipotent. All that is, depends on him for existence. The universe and humankind are his creations. There is an infinite qualitative distinction between God and humankind. The Qur'an warns repeatedly against associating any other being with God. Allah has no equal or partners.

> He is God alone, God the Undivided.
> He does not beget and He is not begotten.
> There is none coequal with him.
>
> (Surah 112)

Traditionally Muslims have ascribed ninety-nine 'beautiful names' to Allah, some found in the Qur'an and some handed down by tradition. The Muslim rosary with its ninety-nine beads is used to bring these to mind. The most important of these beautiful names are the assertions that God is compassionate and God is merciful. Next in importance are the paired names, 'the First and Last': 'the Outward and the Inward'. Among other names are 'the Self-Existent', 'the Giver of Life', 'the Provider', 'the Recorder', and interestingly, 'the One who leads astray'.

Angels

Angels are frequently mentioned in the Qur'an, where they are described as 'messengers of Allah'. They are special creations of God, made of light, charged with specific functions by him. They watch over humans and guard against harm. Two recording angels attend every person. One on the right records good deeds and words; one on the left records bad evil deeds and words. Angels neither eat nor drink and are neither male nor female. They do not have free will; their defining characteristic is complete obedience to God. Their time is spent praising and worshipping God or carrying out his commands.

The books of God

Muslims believe that Allah revealed his will to humans through prophets and through sacred books. Of these books only four now remain: the Taurah (Torah), given to Moses; the Zabur (Psalms), given to David; the Injil (Gospel), given to Jesus and the Qur'an, given to Muhammad. It is claimed that the Jews and Christians, described jointly as people of the Book (*ahl-al-kitab*), changed and distorted their scriptures, so Allah sent the Qur'an as the final revelation for all humankind.

The prophets

God communicates his will for human beings through his chosen spokesmen, the prophets: no female prophets are mentioned in the Qur'an. They instruct the people how to live and worship in accordance with God's command. The Qur'an refers to twenty-five prominent prophets by name; most of this group are also characters in the Judaeo-Christian Scriptures. According to the Qur'an, Allah has sent prophets to every nation and people, to instruct them in obedience, so that on the day of judgement nobody will be able to say that he did not have the opportunity to hear about God. The message of the prophets is that God is one and should be obeyed.

Belief in life after death

The Qur'an teaches that life on earth is temporary and is a preparation for life beyond the grave. There will be a final judgement, after the world has ended, when Allah will judge the dead on the basis of their deeds during life on earth: the good (those whose good deeds outweigh their bad deeds) will gain admittance to Paradise; the evil (those whose bad deeds outweigh their good deeds) will be cast into hell.

The five pillars of Islam

Islam is a practical religion and its emphasis falls on obedience to Allah. Accordingly, God has provided a practical programme to be implemented in daily life that reinforces right conduct and provides a bulwark against temptation and the wiles of Satan. There are traditionally five duties to be observed by Muslims – five 'pillars' upon which true religion rests.

The declaration of faith (shahada)

The first duty of a Muslim is to declare his or her belief that 'there is no God but Allah and Muhammad is the Prophet of God'. To affirm this declaration in front of witnesses identifies one as a member of the community of believers (Umma). This affirmation is incorporated into the five daily prayers of Muslims and for this reason it is often said to be the most used creed in the world.

Prayer (salat)

Prayer is central to the daily life of the Muslim and must be preceded by ritual washing (wudu). There are five compulsory daily prayers – at dawn, noon, mid-afternoon, sunset, and late evening. On each occasion a set cycle of words along with an accompanying ritual involving gestures and movements is used (each individual cycle is called a rakat). Prayers are said in Arabic. Muslim men are required to attend the mosque on Fridays for prayer and to hear a sermon. Women and men are typically segregated.

The practice of giving (zakat)

Although some commentators refer to Zakat as the practice of 'charity', this is not strictly correct. Charity is that which goes beyond the contribution of Zakat. By contrast, Zakat is compulsory. Muslims are expected to give two and a half per cent of their disposable income to the relief of poverty. There is a different rate for agricultural products and livestock.

Traditionally Zakat was collected by the government as an official tax, but nowadays it is a voluntary contribution.

Fasting (sawm)

During the month of Ramadan, all adult Muslims (male and female) must abstain from all food, drink and conjugal relations from sunrise to sunset. Travellers and sick people can defer sawm during Ramadan and make up for it later in the year. Some groups such as children, the elderly and pregnant women are exempt from observing Sawm. Islam follows a lunar calendar so the month of Ramadan and fasting moves around the seasons and one can imagine the self-discipline involved when Ramadan coincides with the hottest months of the year in Middle-Eastern countries.

Pilgrimage (Hajj)

Mecca is the first holy city of Islam and all Muslims are expected (financial circumstances and health allowing) to visit as pilgrims. Muslims believe that the Kaaba in Mecca was originally built by Adam and that later it was the site where in faithfulness to Allah Abraham was willing to offer his son, Ishmael as a sacrifice. When Muhammad and his followers entered Mecca in triumph 1n 630 CE, they cleared the Kaaba of idols and re-consecrated it to the true worship of Allah. A man who has performed the Hajj may dye his beard yellow or orange and may wear a white skull cap. These marks then become a visible symbol of his spirituality and commitment to Allah. He is known as a 'hajji'.

4.1   A VISION OF SALVATION

The way to salvation in Islam is the way of obedience. God loves and pardons those who obey his will, as it is revealed in the Qur'an and in the traditions of Islam. Individuals have freedom to choose whether to serve God or to disobey him. Each person chooses for himself or herself. The Christian notion of original sin is absent from Islam, as is any emphasis upon the sacrificial death of one for another, as in Christ dying for the sins of others. Of course, God is gracious and merciful, in that he could choose to condemn humankind, but has chosen otherwise.

God provides guidance to those who choose to listen and obey. If individuals follow the teaching of Islam then they will be 'saved'. Belief alone is not enough, there must be real commitment to and practice of the teachings of Islam, as revealed in the lives of the prophets, particularly Muhammad, and supremely in the Qur'an: the five pillars should be practised and the example of the prophet Muhammad followed. In submission to God and the teaching of his prophets, peace is found. Those who refuse to surrender to Allah's will and teaching cannot experience peace, but instead bring themselves under condemnation. The unfaithful are condemned to hell and exclusion from God's presence and grace.

According to Muslim tradition, after death two angels visit the dead in their graves and question them on the principles by which they have lived and acted. The hour of the final judgement, however, is known only to God. Its approach will be marked by signs in the heavens and on the earth. Antichrist will appear, only to be defeated by Jesus, who will affirm the faith of Islam. On the third blast of a mighty trumpet the dead will arise to face the judgement of God and his recording angels. All will pass over the abyss of hell by the bridge of as-Sirat, 'finer than a hair and sharper than a sword's edge'. The righteous cross it to paradise, the wicked fall from it into hell. There is debate among Islamic teachers whether all Muslims will enter paradise or not. Some hold that ultimately all those who practice Islam, however falteringly, will gain paradise. The majority of teachers hold that only those whose good deeds outnumber their evil deeds will gain paradise.

Although there is a strong emphasis in Islam on the freedom of individuals to choose whether to obey Allah or not, there is equally an emphasis on the sovereignty of God who rules over all, and this in turn tends to support a strong belief in predestination – the view that all one's actions are ordained by God and that God chooses the path that each will follow. Such a conviction tends to compromise belief in individual freedom, and has given rise to numerous debates between the different philosophical schools of Islam. All affirm, however, that it is the duty of each individual to follow God and his teachings; to fail in this duty is to deserve condemnation by God.

Exaltation of the sovereignty of God has clear implications on the relationship between the human and the divine in Islam. Allah is 'most great'. He is omnipotent, omniscient and eternal. He changes not and is unaffected by the vicissitudes of human history. He created the world and the universe, and directs all things according to his sovereign will and plan. His commands come to pass and all follow the path ordained by him. Some Muslim philosophers taught that such is God's transcendence that nothing positive can be said of him. God is mysterious and human language is entirely inadequate to express his greatness and majesty. The cardinal sin in Islam is the sin of *shirk*, that is, the sin of associating any other (so-called) god or being with the true God. There is an unbridgeable gulf between God and all other creatures. It is for this reason that Muslims reject the deity of Christ. God could not by his nature become a human being, limited in space and time. There is no equivocation about the humanity of Muhammad. He is not divine and although his life is exemplary in every way, he remains most emphatically a human being who relied upon God's grace in living a life of obedience.

Allah is to be worshipped and praised: although petition has a place in Islam it is not a major component in prayer. Prayer is chiefly a means of bringing our wills into agreement with God's will. By prayer we obey and honour God. The notion of a personal relationship with God is absent from much of Islam. I say much and not all because there is a tradition of mysticism within Islam that expressly focuses on the nearness of God.

This is the Sufi tradition, so called because of the rough woollen robes (*suf* in Arabic) worn by early Muslim ascetics who renounced the ordinary world of commerce and industry in order to gain direct experience of God. The chief characteristics of Sufism are common to mystics of different religions: a disciplined life of ascetic obedience, detachment from the world, the practice of devotional exercises, and so on. Traditionally, Muslim mystics have been treated with suspicion by the spokesmen for 'orthodoxy' and some in the past, most notably Al-Hallaj (died 922CE), were executed for identifying themselves too closely with God (Al-Hallaj is reputed to have said 'I am the truth').

4.2   THE COMMUNITY OF BELIEVERS

The notion of community is central to Islam. In Medina, Muhammad forged his followers into a single community, the Umma, charged with the two-fold mission of following the teaching of the prophet and of extending the rule of Allah to all peoples and tribes. The Umma does not take its name from its founder or any event in the early history of Islam. It is the community of Allah. There is no priesthood within Islam and there are no distinctions of status based upon class, race, ethnicity or colour, a point dramatically illustrated by the fact that all pilgrims to Mecca wear simple white garments. Muslims are to regard themselves as members of one family: the Qur'an states that 'believers are naught else than brothers' (Qur'an 49:10). Religious loyalty takes precedence over tribal and group loyalties. The oneness of the community witnesses to the oneness of God. All men and women are equal before Allah and there is no intermediary to supplicate on behalf of others. Allah's command and counsel order the life of the community. What God has revealed as good for the community, shall always remain good, and what he has forbidden shall always remain forbidden. This means that the

Muslim community promotes virtue and abhors vice. Of the virtues, justice is regarded as the most important and the community of Allah is to be distinguished from other communities by its focus on justice. In the *Hadith*, the sacred tradition, it is recorded that one of the noblest acts of striving for God (the word for striving in Islam is *'jihad'*) is to speak the word of justice to an unjust leader. The Umma cannot authorise any changes to God's revealed law: its task is to apply the law and to live by it. Perhaps of all religions, Islam has been most successful in instilling a sense of common religious identity among its adherents. Common patterns of prayer and worship coupled with a remarkable degree of uniformity of belief have combined to produce a shared sense of religious citizenship.

The Umma is ordered and regulated by the 'revealed law', the *Sharia* of God. Regulations for the life of the community occur in the Qur'an, but they cover only a fraction of the issues faced by Muslims as Islamic rule spread and new groups and tribes were incorporated into the Umma. The issue became how to extend and formulate the law so that it would be applicable to new situations and contexts. Within a short time of Muhammad's death a number of law schools had been established in prominent cities with the aim of clarifying and expounding the principles and application of God's law. Naturally, the Qur'an was given a pre-eminent position, but importance was also attached to the example of the prophet and his teachings – the sacred traditions or Hadith of the prophet. In order to extend the applicability of God's law to new situations there was also recourse to the principles of analogy (*qiyas*) and consensus (*ijma*). The combination of Qur'an, Hadith, ijma, and qiyas has been used by Islamic scholars or jurists to create the immensely detailed body of rules and regulations known as the Sharia. It regulates every aspect of a Muslim's public and personal life, and every aspect of government in an Islamic state. There are four different schools of interpretation of Islamic law, though they all agree on the fundamentals of Islam: Hanafi, Maliki, Shafii and Hanbali.

If one asks where does authority lie in Islam, the straightforward answer is that it resides in the Sharia. There is no formally instituted body or spokesperson empowered to articulate an 'official' Islamic view comparable to that of the papacy and the Pope within Catholicism. Muslims pride themselves in not having adopted a hierarchical system of authority: the truth is discovered by going back to the original sources of Islam and by seeking consensus with fellow Muslims. Nevertheless, we need to be realistic about the nature of agreement that exists between Muslims. Like all other religions there have been divisions and schisms. Of these the most important is the division between the Sunni and the Shi'a. Our account of Islam up to now has effectively been an account of the Sunni tradition, which incorporates about 90 per cent of all Muslims. It defers to the authority and judgements of the traditional law schools. Shi'a Islam is much less unified and allows a much stronger role to charismatic religious leaders and reformers.

The roots of the division go back to the period of time following the death of the prophet Muhammad. It originated in a dispute over leadership and who was properly entitled to lead the community. Upon Muhammad's death, Abu-Bakr, a close friend and an original convert from Mecca, was appointed as successor (Caliph), charged with the responsibility of ordering and leading the community (a definitive version of the Qur'an was not available at this time). He in turn was succeeded by Umar, who was succeeded by Uthman, and he in turn by Ali. The first four caliphs are referred to as the 'rightly guided'. Ali was Muhammad's adopted son and married to the prophet's daughter, and for these reasons there were those who regarded him as the rightful heir to Muhammad. But his appointment was controversial and one of Uthman's kinsmen, Mu'awiya opposed him with an army in battle. The result was indecisive and both agreed to arbitration. In disgust at Ali's acceptance of arbitration some of his followers deserted him, and shortly afterwards he was murdered while at prayer by a former supporter. Mu'awiya gained the position of Caliph, though the 'party of Ali' (*Shiat Ali*, hence Shi'a) contended that this was because he had promised to revert the Chaliphate to the family of Ali at the end of his reign. By the time of his death, however, Ali's first son, Hasan, had already died (possibly as a result of poisoning) and on his deathbed Mu'awiya appointed his own son, Yazid as heir and Caliph. Ali's second son Husain, with a small force of supporters, rose up in rebellion, only to be slaughtered by a much larger force.

Those who supported the family of Ali's claim to become Caliph developed their own tradition of Islam, far removed from the centres of Sunni power and influence. Shi'a Islam focuses around charismatic leaders who expound and interpret the Qur'an. It claims to preserve different traditions of the practice and example of the prophet Muhammad; though in fairness it shares many beliefs and practices with Sunni Islam, the five pillars, for example. There is a strong expectation among Shi'ites that a future leader or imam will emerge to restore the fortunes of the family of Ali. (In Sunni Islam the term 'imam' simply refers to the accredited teacher and leader in the mosque).

4.3   A CELEBRATING TRADITION

Although the Qur'an does not prescribe any ritual for the celebration of a new addition to a family, tradition requires that a number of customs be observed. After the birth, when the child has been properly washed and dressed, he or she will be carried by the midwife to the assembly of male relatives and friends. The head of the family then recites the 'call to prayer' in the child's right ear (the *adhan*) and the command to rise and worship (the *iqamah*) in the left ear. After the tradition of the prophet Muhammad, a tiny piece of sugar, date or honey is placed in the child's mouth by the oldest and most respected relative, perhaps the grandfather or uncle. This symbolises making the child 'sweet', obedient and kind. After this, prayers are said for the health and prosperity of the child.

Seven days after birth comes the *Aqiqah* ceremony, when relatives and friends come to a prepared feast and the baby is named. The baby's head is shaved, and by tradition the same weight as the hair in gold or silver is set aside for the poor. This is followed by a sacrifice of thanksgiving – two animals are offered for a boy and one for a girl. For Muslims, as for religious people everywhere, a new life is a gift from God and so thanks should be expressed. The meat is cooked and shared with visitors, with some usually set aside for the poor. The child is given his name, frequently a name with religious connotations, such as Abdullah, 'Servant of God' or Abdul Rahman, 'Servant of the merciful'. If the child is a boy he will also be circumcised at this time. *Khitan* or circumcision is required for Muslims, and should not be delayed unless there are health problems. On the child's fourth birthday comes *bismillah*, the occasion when he is taught to recite and learn a short passage from the Qur'an – 'In the name of God, the Compassionate, the Merciful'. The child's formal education into Islam has now begun. In a Muslim country this education will continue in day school, and in non-Islamic countries religious education will be pursued in a school attached to the mosque, a *madrasah*, after normal school hours.

The mosque plays an important role within the Muslim community. It is a place of prayer and education, and it also serves as a centre for the community. Although marriages in the West are frequently conducted in the mosque, this is not strictly required. Marriages are arranged by the family to ensure that an appropriate partner is found. The marriage ceremony itself is a simple affair. The bride need not attend; instead she may send two witnesses to attest to her agreement. The ceremony takes only a few minutes: a number of readings from the Qur'an, the exchange of vows and prayers. The imam or official religious teacher need not be present. The role of the imam is that of teacher and community leader, he is not regarded as possessing any special powers or privileges. Any faithful member of the community can officiate at weddings and funerals. There is no priesthood in Islam.

The aim of religious education in Muslim countries is to initiate the individual into the beliefs, customs and traditions of Islam. There are special food laws to be obeyed – alcohol is forbidden and meat must be ritually slaughtered. Special festivals also serve to stimulate and encourage faith. We have already noted that Muslims follow a lunar calendar and as a consequence the festivals move around the seasons. The Muslim word for a festival is 'id' or 'eid', taken from an Arabic word meaning 'returning at regular intervals'. Festivals are distinguished as minor or major. Maulid-an-Nabi, the birthday of the prophet Muhammad, Lailat-ul-Qadr, the Night of Power, celebrating the revelation of the first verses of the Qur'an to Muhammad, and Lailat-ul-Miraj, commemorating Muhammad's miraculous journey to Jerusalem and his ascent to the presence of God, are all minor festivals. Eid-ul-Fitr and Eid-ul-Adha are major festivals.

Eid-ul-Fitr is the feast that marks the end of the month long Ramadan fast. On the last evening of the fast, Muslims will often assemble outside to celebrate the sight of the full moon in the sky (the Muslim day begins at sunset). It is a time of great joy and celebration. Decorations are hung in homes and cards are sent to friends and relatives. The next morning all the family will dress in their best clothes and attend the mosque or if the crowd is too big then all will go to a park or civic amenity where the celebrations begin in worship and prayer to Allah. Prayers will be recited and the imam will address the crowd. Alms will be collected for the poor and family members will return to their parents' home to join in the celebration. After mosque attendance, there will be a grand meal and presents will be distributed, particularly to children. In the afternoon, it is also customary to visit the cemetery in order to remember the loved ones who are divided from their families in death.

The feast of Eid-ul-Adha is not only the climax of the Hajj pilgrimage, but also the main festival of the Islamic year. It takes place in the month of Hajj, two months after the end of Ramadan. It commemorates the triumph of Ibrahim's (Abraham's) faith over the temptation of the devil and illustrates his complete submission to God. Ibrahim had a vivid dream in which he was instructed by God to sacrifice his only son Ishmael. On awaking he told Ishmael of his dream, who encouraged him to do as God had commanded. Both set off for Mina, the place of sacrifice. On the way the devil tempted Ibrahim in different ways: he suggested that God would never command such an act; that Hagar, Ibrahim's maid-servant and Ishmael's mother, could never bear such a tragedy; and that Ibrahim was losing his mind and should not trust the revelation from God. With fortitude Ibrahim resisted the devil, and at the place of sacrifice, just as he was about to offer up Ishmael, God intervened and provided a sacrifice of his own. As a reward for Ibrahim's faithfulness, his first wife, Sarah gave birth to a son – Isaac. Ishmael became the founder of the Arab tribes and nation, Isaac became the founder of the Jews.

For Muslims Eid-ul-Adha symbolizes their submission to God. Every Muslim participates in the festival, not just those on pilgrimage – though it does have added significance for those who celebrate it as pilgrims in the place where the original events took place. It is an occasion for the extended family to come together and reflect upon their religious commitment. A special meal is prepared and gifts are distributed. An animal will be chosen for sacrifice – a sheep, goat, cow or camel may be offered. Traditionally, the responsibility for slaughter rested with the father of the family or a senior member of the extended family. The throat of the animal must be cut and the blood allowed to drain away. Meat from an animal killed in the correct way is called *halal* or 'permitted'. Prayers are said throughout the proceedings. In non-Muslim countries it is expected that animals will be ritually slaughtered in an abattoir.

4.4   CHALLENGES TO THE TRADITION

Within all religions there is great variety, and the features of Islam that attract most attention from Western eyes may not be the features that Muslims themselves identify as significant. From a Muslim perspective the most obvious feature of Islam in the modern world is its vitality and confidence. Islam is a missionary religion with a divine mandate to convert the world to Islam. Its attractions are obvious: a clear and unequivocal religious message, a call to moral purity, and a community of believers to offer support and encouragement. Many Muslims view modern Western society as spiritually and morally bankrupt. High levels of divorce, the practice of abortion, rampant materialism and individualism all witness to a society that has lost its way. Islam offers itself as a realistic spiritual option with the potential to bring a new sense of moral purpose and urgency to the West.

Yet for those who do not belong to the Muslim tradition, the promise of Islam is a mixed blessing. The renewal of society is predicated on acceptance of both a religious and a *political* message, for in Islam there is no distinction between religion and politics. Islam provides a blueprint for society, where the Western distinction between the sacred and the profane is abrogated. The religious message of Islam is also a political message. For many Muslims, it is only when the law of Sharia is adopted by the state that the prospect of living a truly religious life becomes realisable. The state and its institutions should support the teaching and practice of Islam. In Islam there is no private dimension of life to which God's law does not apply, and more controversially, to which God's law should not be applied by the state. Such a position is greeted with some alarm by non-Muslims, who view it as a form of totalitarianism that is opposed to the principles of liberal democracy and the restrictions on state power that follow from liberal commitments to individual rights, such as freedom of religion and the freedom to formulate and follow one's own conception of the good. Liberals object to the suggestion that the state should enforce religious conformity on all its subjects. There is much that could be said on this debate and there are examples of democratic states within the Arab world, but their existence is controversial and always vulnerable to the charge that the exclusive nature of Islamic truth and practice has been compromised. The appeal of fundamentalism within Islam remains powerful and attractive.

This tension between the principles of liberal democracy and the principles of Islam directs us to a deeper and more fundamental source of tension and controversy within Islam, namely how is the absolute truth of the Qur'an to be maintained and interpreted in the modern world. The Qur'an is regarded by Muslims as the literal and infallible Word of God. It reflects God's wishes and intention on every subject on which it speaks: the principles of justice and appropriate forms of punishment, the ordering of community life and economic relations, the behaviour appropriate to different roles, and so on. Tension emerges when it is realised that many of the prescriptions for action and behaviour conflict with modern sensibilities. Should particularly harsh punishments as prescribed in the Qur'an and in the Sharia law be imposed on those who transgress? Should Muslims have the right to renounce Islam and embrace a different religion without the fear of punishment and even death? Should Muslim women be allowed to marry non-Muslims? To what extent, if at all, should liberal democracies take account of Muslim law and custom, for example, permitting a man to marry up to four wives at one time, permitting young women to wear traditional forms of dress in a public environment such as a school or a hospital? Those who believe that the content of the Qur'an is inviolate and relevant without revision to all societies are now usually referred to as 'fundamentalists' (the term of course originally referred to early-twentieth-century American Protestants who contended for the 'fundamentals' of their faith). 'Back to the Qur'an' is their rallying call and mandate. Other Muslims seek some kind of reconciliation between Islam and modernity. The challenge for those of this persuasion is how to distinguish between that which can be revised and superseded from that which is essential and properly determinative of the tradition. Is it possible to combine faithfulness to Islam with faithfulness to liberal principles of justice, democracy and rational criticism?

The all-embracing nature of Islam as a way of life naturally raises important critical questions, some of which we have briefly aired, but it also raises practical questions. Ideally, Islam should be practised in a Muslim state that supports the beliefs and institutions of Islam. But what of those Muslims who live in states where they are in the minority and where their concerns and difficulties are given scant attention? What provisions are made for Muslim employees to attend the mosque on Friday or even to allow Muslims to practise the daily round of prayers and devotions that are expected by their religion? How are Muslim sensitivities respected in the public realm of education, welfare and law? It is difficult for those who are not Muslims to appreciate the difficulties they face in a post-Christian, liberal, permissive society. The real challenge for Muslims is how to reinterpret Islam so that it both constitutes a challenge to the secular world while not posing a threat to the freedom of those who choose not to embrace Islam. The Christian dialogue with modernity and its exaltation of critical reason has been going on for centuries, the dialogue of Islam with modernity is only beginning.

5

Hinduism

Just as the flowing rivers disappear in the ocean,
Casting off name and form, even so the knower,
Freed from name and form, attains to the divine
Brahman, higher than the high.

Mundaka Upanishad

Hinduism is the name given to a family of religious beliefs and practices that began and still flourish in India today. To speak of Hinduism as a religion may be confusing in two different ways. First, Hinduism embraces all of life, from explicit advice on how the divine is to be worshipped to rules that govern the kinds of food it is appropriate to eat or clothes to wear: in the West we are accustomed to confining religion to a narrow sphere of influence. Secondly, there is no clearly defined religious authority that determines the boundaries between belief and non-belief. Some Hindus believe in God, some do not, and some believe that worship of God is indicative of a rudimentary stage of religious awareness. Hinduism has been described as a loose confederation of cults and religious groups that mutually acknowledge each other as existing within the one evolving tradition, but without any common beliefs or practices. Nehru once remarked that the only idea common to

Hindus was the idea that the cow is sacred! Hinduism is as much a cultural way of life as it is a religion, and for this reason our Western habit of distinguishing religious activities from non-religious activities does not fit the cultural reality of Hinduism. For Hindus in India, Hinduism is an inextricable part of their existence, a complete approach to life that involves social class, earning a living, family, politics and diet, in addition to the things Westerners view as religious.

The word 'Hinduism' is derived from a Persian name for India. 'Hindu' in Persian was originally the name of the River Indus. The Persians called the country around and beyond the Indus, Hindustan ('the place of the Indus'), and called its people Hindu. In early usage this meant that the terms applied to all those who lived beyond the Indus. In the early nineteenth century it was still possible to speak of a Hindu Christian, meaning a Christian of Indian origin and cultural background. Traditionally Indians referred to their system of beliefs and practices as Sanatana Dharma, the 'Eternal Way or Order'. This designation underlines the fact that Hinduism traces its ancestry far back in history; it is the religious path that has developed and evolved on the Indian sub-continent for over four millennia.

An overview of Hinduism

We have already spoken of development within Hinduism, and there has been considerable development over the centuries, as one family of ideas gave way to another. Nevertheless, it would be a mistake to think of these developments as progressive and linear, as if earlier ideas and beliefs were always displaced from the religious imagination and superseded by ideas of later origin. This has not been the case; rather beliefs from an earlier historical period co-exist today alongside much later beliefs. Often these later beliefs seem to conflict with what was affirmed in earlier periods. But conforming religion to the principles of strict logic and coherence has never been a characteristic mark of religious communities. Religious believers might legitimately retort of course that the attempt to define the divine in human terms necessarily requires a certain stretching of human language and our traditional categories of sense and meaning.

The historical development of Indian religion may fruitfully be compared to a landscape described by a geologist. Different features, rocks, hills, valleys, are visible on the surface. On closer examination strata of different geological ages can be discerned and the data used to reconstruct the geological and geographical history of the region. As the geologist speaks of successive layers or strata of rock laid down during long geological ages, so we can fruitfully speak of successive strata of religion laid down during different phases of Indian history. Modern Hinduism is a combination of beliefs from different periods, combined in odd ways and unrelated in other ways.

The history of Hinduism

Five different historical layers of Indian religion can be identified and distinguished.

Indus Valley Civilisation

The Indus Valley Civilization thrived in Northwest India from the middle of the third millennium BCE to the middle of the second millennium BCE. The civilization had a well-developed culture centred on two major cities, Mohenjo-Daro and Harappa. The language of this civilisation has still to be deciphered. From archaeological evidence we know that these people had a strong belief in the gods and that the practice of meditation, what would later be called yoga, may have been an important part of their religious activities.

The Vedic Period (2000 BCE – 400 BCE)

Indo-Aryans, a nomadic tribe, began to migrate into the Indus Valley area over the period from 2000 BCE to 1500 BCE, and this migration, most archaeologists believe, displaced the original inhabitants of the Indus valley and destroyed their ancient civilisation. The religious scriptures of the Indo-Aryans, which bring together a number of different collections of writings produced over a period of time, serve as the most widely acknowledged basis for Hinduism and are regarded as 'revealed wisdom' by all the different schools of Hinduism. The most important religious writing of this period are the Vedas, of which there are four: the Rig Veda, Yajur Veda, Sama-Veda and the Atharva Veda. The word 'veda' means 'knowledge' and the collections provide classes of priests with the knowledge they needed for their functions in the increasingly elaborate Aryan rituals. The Vedas contain hymns to the gods, sacred mantras or symbolic utterances, descriptions of cures and curses, and elaborate descriptions of sacrifice. The Hindu ideas of *Dharma* (righteousness), *Karma* (every action bears fruit) and *Rita* (cosmic order) are derived from the Vedas, particularly the Rig Veda. The gods were guardians of the cosmic order and so they had to be propitiated by means of sacrifice. The Vedas are said to contain the eternal truths of the religion and are upheld as the supreme authority for Hinduism, even though the teaching of some of the religious groups and philosophical schools within Hinduism seems only contingently and indirectly related to the content of the Vedas.

In time, each of the Vedas came to include subsequent discussions of the nature and purpose of sacrifice and ritual. These discussions are referred to as the Brahmanas. In this body of literature priesthood is assumed to be powerful and the four stages of life were formulated: the student, householder, forest dweller and ascetic stages. New doctrines such as that of transmigration and caste are also introduced. The Brahmanas declared that all beings must be reborn over and over again, in an endless cycle. From transmigration arose the need to find release (*Moksha*). The production of the Brahmanas was followed by the production of the Aranyakas and Upanishads, philosophical and mystical texts dealing with the quest for *atman*, that is, knowledge of the true self. It was during this period, particularly the period of the writing of the Upanishads, roughly the eighth century to fourth century BCE that the foundations of Hinduism were solidly laid. Gods and sacrifices receded into the background and the quest for self-realisation became pre-eminent. The Upanishads contain one central theme, namely, the unity of the individual soul or atman with the one impersonal and absolute universal spirit – *Brahman*.

The sacred literature of the Vedas and the bodies of commentary material referred to in our discussion are regarded as *shruti*, 'that which is heard or divinely revealed'. It is distinguished from later religious writings that are described as *smriti*, 'that which is remembered or handed down'. In this category is included the Mahabarata, of which the Bhagavad Gita is a part, and the Ramayana (see below).

The Epic and Classical Periods (400 BCE – 600 CE)
Throughout the epic period, the Indo-Aryans increasingly settled into towns and cities, and ceased to be a nomadic people. They settled mainly in the Plains of North India, and they related their religion to that of the indigenous people they had come to dominate. To this period belongs the two greatest Hindu epics, the Ramayana, 'The Story of Rama', and the Mahabarata, the 'Great Story of the War of the Bharatas'. Both epics concern themselves with the royal heroes' duties to maintain the harmonious realm of dharma and the Vedic rituals and religious practices that ensure it. The Bhagavad Gita, the 'Song of the Lord', is the most popular of the Hindu Scriptures. The Gita is famous because it touches on the main concerns of the central beliefs of Hinduism – dharma, class distinctions and moksha. In addition, it introduces a number of important new doctrines, namely *Bhakti* (devotion to God) and *Avatara* (manifestations of God). The Laws of Manu, which

provide instruction on the ideal nature of society, were also a product of the epic period. The Law books were primarily concerned with maintaining social stability through a hierarchically arranged class system.

The Medieval Period (600 – 1800 CE)

The medieval period in Hinduism is primarily characterized by the rise of devotional movements, the systematization of Hindu philosophy into six schools, and the rise of Tantrism. With the rise and spread of devotional (bhakti) movements, came the rise of temples as important religious centres in Hinduism. The mythology of the deities worshipped at these temples became systematised in a genre of works called the Puranas or 'Stories of old'. The second major development in this period was the formalisation of the six schools of Hindu philosophy: *Nyaya* ('Analysis'), *Vaisheshika* ('the School of Individual Characteristics'), *Sankhya* ('the Count'), *Yoga* ('spiritual discipline'), *Mimamsa* ('Enquiry' or 'Thought'), and finally, *Vedanta* ('the End of the Vedas'). These philosophies, ranging from non-theism to monotheism to dualism, emphasised different ways of obtaining liberation. The third major development, the *Tantras*, are the scriptures of those who worship *Shakti*, the supreme being personified as a goddess. The Tantras, 'Rules or Rituals', claimed to introduce methods that could lead directly to liberation without *traditional* ritual practices. They instead offered a variety of rituals that employ mantras, mandalas, and yogic techniques. Through their complex rituals and theologies, the Tantras, together with the Puranas, had a significant influence on popular religion throughout the medieval period.

The Modern Period (1800 – Present)

The modern period of Hinduism continues to be heavily influenced by contact with Western cultures. With the arrival of Western powers in India in the eighteenth century,

Westerners and some Hindus alike began to express criticism towards the some elements of the Hindu tradition. In response, a number of reform movements emerged, two of which are particularly important. Both attempted to recover the essentials of Hinduism while doing away with unwanted and criticised excess. Ram Mohan Roy (1774–1833) founded the first of these movements, Brahmo Samaj, a school of rational theism purely based on the Upanishads. In contrast, Swami Dayananda (1824–1883), founder of the Arya Samaj, found the essence of Hinduism in the Vedas. Furthermore, he denounced idol worship as well as the discriminatory caste system. Although neither movement gained a considerably large audience, they succeeded in contributing to the independence movement of the nineteenth and twentieth centuries. The two most famous leaders of the independence movement were Bal Gangadhar Tilak (1859-1920) and Mohandas Karamachand Gandhi (1869-1948). Both leaders regarded the Bhagavad Gita as central to their teaching and attempted to reconcile the tension between renunciation of the world and support for social justice in the world.

In the modern period the various insights, practices and procedures of the former periods are combined and amalgamated with local indigenous traditions to produce a federation of cults and customs which are subsumed under the designation Hinduism. Central to the lived experience of many Hindus, particularly in the villages and small towns, are the twin concepts of purity and pollution. If one adheres to the rules of class and caste and fulfils one's duties as prescribed in the sacred literature then purity is achieved. But if one fails in one's duties, then one is polluted. In this case sacred rituals and devotions are to be performed, so that the evil consequences of pollution may be averted. Consequently, the daily life of many is governed by the need to escape pollution and retain ritual and religious purity; only the pure can experience the divine and receive favour.

Central beliefs

Gods, goddesses and brahman
Belief in the existence of gods and goddesses has been a strong
feature of Hindu religion, though the precise sense in which
the reality and existence of the gods is to be interpreted is
another matter. Certainly in the Vedas the gods are assumed to
exist, and thus one may properly speak of polytheism, though
even here some caution is needed, because the pattern of
religious devotion is usually that within a particular hymn one
god is regarded as supreme and more powerful than all the rest.
This pattern of devotion still exists today, in that many Hindus
will chose a god to follow and lavish more worship and
attention on him or her than on other gods. The most popular
gods are Vishnu and Shiva; together with Brahma, the three
form a sort of Trinity; Brahma is the principle of creation in the
universe, Vishnu that of preservation, and Shiva that of
destruction. From the viewpoint of worship, however, Brahma
is of little importance, rarely has a temple been dedicated to
him or a group formed in his name. By contrast, Vishnu and
Shiva are deities of the highest order. Vishnu is believed by his
followers to have descended to earth on different occasions to
restore righteousness and order, and he is often worshipped
under the form of one of these 'appearances', particularly as
Krishna, the hero of the Bhagavad Gita. The worship of
Krishna is associated with the devotional movement, the bhakti
movement, which looks upon devotion to God and God's grace
as a means of achieving salvation (moksha). Shiva, by contrast,
is the god of chaos and destruction. He is associated with death,
ascetic practice and the violent aspects of creation.

Alongside worship of the gods in Hinduism exists a different
tradition of religion, that is, a philosophical form of religion
that looks beyond the gods to a deeper unity within the
universe. This tradition looks to the Upanishads for inspiration
and identifies divine unity behind the multiplicity of deities,

persons and universes. The Upanishads speak of *Tat Tvam Asi*, 'Thou are That', by which it means the soul, atman, is in essence identical with the One, Brahman. This belief is authenticated in mystical experience, where the self becomes one with the Greater Self that is present in all things. This notion of identity is interpreted in different ways within the different schools of devotion and philosophy within Hinduism. The devotional schools regard union with Brahman as union with the divine Lord, a personal union with the godhead; the philosophical schools tend to interpret Brahman as an impersonal force or power within which human personality and separateness is transcended. In such schools devotional worship of the gods is acknowledged as legitimate for those who lack the intellect or temperament to accept the deeper truth that that which is most real is impersonal.

Karma-samsara
Samsara is the belief that the soul (the true self, the atman) goes through a cycle of birth, death, and rebirth. *Karma* is the force or law that determines the quality of each life, depending on how well one has acted in a past life. Karma is the word for 'action', and because each action bears fruit in the sense that consequences follow from it, either good or bad, so the actions of a life bear fruit in a further life. Good actions bear good consequences and evil actions bear bad consequences. The social position one gains at birth is determined by one's actions in a previous existence. The law of karma is regarded as a natural law of justice and is the foundation of moral action and virtue.

Caste
The Indian constitution declares that it is illegal to distinguish between individuals on the basis of caste, yet the concept of caste is deeply interwoven historically into the fabric of Hinduism. The Vedas speak of four different hierarchically

ordered classes (*varnas*) of people, whose origins are traced to
different parts of the body of a mythological first man: the
Brahmin or priestly class comes from the mouth, the Kshatriya
or warrior class from the arms, the Vaishya or merchant class
comes from the thighs, and the Shudra or worker class from the
feet. Only the three top classes are regarded as 'twice-born' and
rituals appropriate to them are excluded to other groups.
Outside the fourfold class distinction lies a further group, who
comprise the lowest level of Hindu society. They are often
referred to as the 'untouchables', though in an effort to elevate
their status Ghandi referred to them as the *Harijan*, 'the
children of God'.

Many earlier commentators on Hinduism use the term class
and caste interchangeably, but more recently some have
preferred to confine use of class to the four traditional orders of
society and to use the term caste to refer to the numerous
distinctions between groups that exist within the broader class
system. Both terms refer to a prescribed social position within a
broader hierarchical arrangement. This prescribed social
position carries implications for the form of worship, dress,
occupation, and marriage partner that one may choose. Other
Hindus will relate to you on the basis of your class and caste. For
some traditional Indian writers the acceptance of caste is the
essence of Hinduism. A Hindu is a Hindu not because he
accepts certain doctrines or performs certain rituals, but because
he is a member of caste. Hence on this definition it is impossible
to become a Hindu, other than by being born into caste.

5.1   A VISION OF SALVATION

The achievement of salvation is the hope of every Hindu, even
though not every Hindu will aim to achieve salvation in his or
her current life-time. Many will aim to cultivate good karma in
this life in the expectation of achieving a better rebirth next
time. With commitment, good deeds and devotion so better

and higher rebirths can be achieved over successive lives until there is a realistic hope of gaining salvation.

The Hindi word for salvation is *moksha*. It is probably best translated into English as 'liberation'. One of the dangers of translating moksha with salvation is that Christian associations are inappropriately read into the original Hindu concept. Although the nature of moksha is subject to different interpretations within the different schools and religious groups within Hinduism, there are two discernable common elements. The first is that moksha is deliverance from the wheel of successive rebirths. The law of karma is overcome and the endless cycle of birth, growth to maturity and death is terminated. The wheel of rebirth stops turning. The second is that moksha is deliverance from ignorance (*advidya*). The essential barrier to moksha is lack of knowledge. Individuals do not recognise the truth and consequently do not follow the path that alone leads to truth. Knowledge leads to liberation as the true nature of the self's identity with the divine is recognised and one begins to live a life according to one's lofty status. This minimum definition of moksha can be expanded in different ways and the different philosophies within Hinduism draw subtle distinction between each other on the basis of their particular interpretation of the experience of liberation.

We have already noted the diversity of ideas of the divine that abound within Hinduism and obviously such diversity is reflected in different concepts of moksha. Where the divine is conceived as personal, as in the Vedas and in some of the Upanishads, then moksha is essentially union with one's chosen Lord. The union with god that is experienced in life is consummated after death, when the devotee enters heaven and enjoys the divine presence forever. Where the divine is conceived as impersonal then moksha is understood as absorption and loss of identity within the One, which includes within itself the universe and all that is: the individual self, atman, is identical with the Greater self, Brahman. One of the images that is used to describe this experience is that of the water of a river merging and losing its separate identity in the water of the great Ocean. Brahman becomes all in all: the self become one with all that is.

Hindus distinguish between three different paths or ways of achieving liberation: the path of works (*Karma-marga*), the path of knowledge (*Jnana-marga*), and the path of devotion (*Bhakti-marga*). All three paths can claim support from the sacred scriptures of Hinduism. They should not be regarded as separate or exclusive, in the sense that to follow one path excludes any role for the beliefs and practices associated with any other. Hindus typically combine the different paths within an overall emphasis upon one practical path.

Karma-marga

According to the Vedas, karma-marga is the chief path to salvation. Moksha is gained by 'right action'. In the Vedas, right action refers principally to the offering of gifts and prayers to the gods and the proper performance of the sacrificial rites. With the rise of the Brahmin priestly class the importance attached to sacrifice as a means of securing moksha became even greater. At this stage in Vedic spirituality little attention was given to the moral content of religion: religion and morality were not closely connected. This situation has changed by the time the Upanishads were written. The concept of dharma as righteous acts now comes to the fore and consequently dharma comes to include moral as well as social, religious and economic elements.

Jnana-marga

Jnana-marga is the way of knowledge, but knowledge in this context is not to be regarded as intellectual knowledge, but rather experiential knowledge. In a significant number of the Upanishads there is a reaction against the performance of religious duties, particularly those associated with sacrifice and the performance of intricate rituals as enjoined by the Vedas. Meditation and the search for experiential knowledge replace worship and sacrifice. Indeed, according to some passages in the Upanishads, true sacrifice is the disciplined life of the student of sacred knowledge. To follow this path to moksha requires not only intense study, but ascetic discipline typically involving renunciation of one's family and material possessions. This is the way of the wandering holy-man (*sannyasin*), who retreats from the activities of ordinary life to pursue self-discipline and the practice of yoga – a structured series of mental and physical exertions.

Bhakti-marga

Bhakti-marga is the way of worship and devotion. The focus is upon god, who is looked upon as active and gracious. Dedication to god in worship and devotion wins favour, not just for spiritual ends but for worldly ends as well, say a suitable marriage partner or a propitious business venture. In the Bhagavad Gita seekers of moksha are instructed to devote themselves to Krishna, the personal manifestation of the God Vishnu: they are to love and trust him. The means of achieving liberation is ultimately God's grace, but looked at from the perspective of this world, it is devotion. Devotion properly understood, according to the Gita, is the fulfilment of social duty, Upanishadic knowledge and Vedic ritual obligation. Not everyone can be a priest or learned seer, but everyone can know the Lord through devotion. God in his mercy will accept us if we turn to him in devotion and faith. All our actions and duties should be dedicated to him. Krishna speaks thus:

> Quickly I come to those who offer me every action,
> Worship me only…
> With devotion undaunted.
>
> Because they love me they are my bondsmen,
> And I shall save them from mortal sorrow,
> And all the waves of life's deathly ocean.

For those who follow with rigour the jnana-marga the body is to be disciplined and even punished, so that one's spiritual nature can be nurtured. The image of the person (*purusha*) imprisoned and entangled in nature (*prakriti*) is often used to describe the human situation. The real self is one with god or Brahman, yet the true nature of our human identity is hidden from us. We are ignorant of our true selves. The world is illusory (*maya*) and we lavish time and energy on worldly pursuits that are of no abiding significance and positively distract us from pursuit of that which is most real and permanent – the true self that is at one with the Eternal Spirit. Atman is identical with Brahman, or in the theistic traditions, atman is one with his Lord.

5.2   THE COMMUNITY OF BELIEVERS

There is no recognised central religious authority in Hinduism. The question 'Who speaks for Hinduism?' has no straightforward or uncontroversial answer. One commentator has remarked that there are as many Hinduisms as there are Hindus. Authority resides in the Vedas and the body of interpretative material that was added by subsequent generations. (This formal appeal to the authority of the Vedas serves to exclude Buddhism as a recognised school within Hinduism: the Buddha's rejection of the Vedas and the propriety of caste distinctions place him outside the Hindu family of faiths.) Philosophical Hinduism with its elevation of spiritual reality and depreciation of worldly existence contrasts with popular Hinduism where rituals and fear of pollution determine daily existence. We can speak of the authority of tradition in Hinduism, provided we acknowledge that there are numerous traditions upon which Hindus can draw. The all-encompassing nature of Hinduism allows that there are many ways to the truth, and each person must choose his own. The learned sage may follow a different path from the simple believer. This position is consistent with Hinduism's emphasis upon personal experience. Authority resides with the individual who has experiential knowledge not with the individual who has intellectual knowledge. Brahman is known in experience. Different paths to truth are appropriate for those of different temperament, personality and aptitude.

If we say that the notion of religious authority in Hinduism is individualistic and diffuse, we immediately have to qualify this by stating that the authority of community is pervasive and important. This qualification reflects the fact that Hinduism embraces all of life. If there is great latitude with regard to (what we in the West would refer to as) religious belief and practice, there is little latitude with regard to social belief and practice. The life of the ordinary Hindu is rule-governed: prescriptions on what one may eat, wear, the company one keeps, the occupations one may pursue, and the religious rituals one should perform are determined by tradition and given religious sanction. Until modern times the influence of caste, with its rules and regulations, ordered the daily life of the Hindu. To rebel against caste was to exclude oneself from the religious community. Disrespect towards parents and the community is much more likely to incur the wrath of other Hindus that the adoption of a critical attitude towards Hindu religious beliefs and practices. In any case the acceptable diversity of belief within Hinduism reduces the possibility of religious conflict and disagreement. Criticism of the social community and disrespect towards its traditions are more serious matters.

5.3   A CELEBRATING TRADITION

Important events in a Hindu's life such as birth, marriage and death are endowed with religious significance and are naturally marked by religious ceremonies and rites.

On the birth of a child, sacred mantras (taken from the Hindu Scriptures) are uttered in the child's ear, who is then given a tiny amount of gold, dipped in honey, to suck. After birth the mother is isolated until she has performed a ritual act of purification and a symbolic mark is made on the child's forehead. The naming ceremony takes place on the twelfth day in the presence of family and relatives. Interestingly, the name is not disclosed earlier, for fear that evil spirits gain influence over the child before ritual protection is gained through scarlet threads that are tied to the body in the ceremony. A piece of gold is also normally given as a present by the family as a symbol of good fortune. The child is formally named by a Brahmin priest. This is followed by party celebrations.

At adolescence a further initiatory rite, the sacred thread ceremony, confers the status of twice born upon those boys who are born into the higher classes. There is regional variation in the age at which this 'sacrament' is administered. The ceremony confers the status of adulthood and marks the beginning of the student stage of life i.e. the stage prior to marriage and family responsibilities. The individual is now entitled to perform worship (*puja*) and to offer sacrifice to the gods; he is also required to observe the rules of purity and class. Hindus interpret the ceremony as a kind of spiritual birth and those to whom it is administrated are called the 'twice born'. A sacred thread is placed over the left shoulder and falls under the right arm to the waist. During the ceremony mantras are recited by the Brahmin priest. In earlier times it was customary for the gift of a cow to be made to the initiate, nowadays other presents are more typically given as tokens of affection and support.

Marriage is also endowed with religious significance. For Hindu men it marks entrance into the householder stage of life and the duty to raise and support a wife and family. Marriages are regarded as bringing two families together, and consequently the families are involved in the choice of a marriage partner for their respective children. Marriages in Hinduism can be very elaborate affairs, with festivities extending over a number of days, though in the West, celebrations are usually kept to a single day. In the past it was usual for the bride and groom not to meet until the day of their wedding. This is not normally the case today; though when a couple do meet before marriage it is usually in the company of others. Before a marriage partner is agreed upon by either family there will a consultation with a priest who will identity on the basis of the couple's date of birth and star sign whether the proposed union will be propitious. The priest will also identify the best dates on which the marriage should be conducted. The ceremony may take place either at the bride's home or in a temple. Vows will be made in Sanskrit, sacred prayers will be said by the priest, and the couple will walk a number of times (sometimes as many as seven) around a sacred fire or flame, on each occasions both touching a stone on the ground symbolising firmness and commitment.

The passage from this world in death is a solemn affair and is marked by a number of religious duties that are performed by the surviving eldest son of the deceased. In India he leads the funeral procession and before lighting the funeral pyre whispers the sacred sound 'Aum' in the ear of the deceased in order to attune him to the Spirit of the universe. In Britain the funeral ceremonies are carried out in a crematorium, and the ashes of the deceased person are sometimes transported back to India to be cast on the waters of the sacred River Ganges.

We have already noted that Hinduism embraces a diversity of traditions and beliefs and there is hardly a day where somewhere in Indian a god or goddess is not being celebrates by a festival in his or her honour. Festivals are a common occurrence, with many confined to tribal or regional areas. There are two main religious calendars that determine festival dates, both combining solar and lunar features; as a consequence festivals do not occur on the same date each year (as far as the Western calendar is concerned). The main religious festivals, which are celebrated throughout the Indian sub-continent and in Indian communities across the world, are the birthday of Lord Rama, the birthday of Lord Krishna, Holi and Divali. As examples we will focus on the celebration of Holi and Divali.

Holi is a spring festival that celebrates the end of the winter months and the advent of new growth and the season of planting. It is celebrated in the month of Phalguna (which falls between February and March in our Western calendar), on the day of a full moon. There are a number of different Hindu stories and myths that relate to the origins of Holi. One story is that the devout youth Prahlad survived being placed on a burning bonfire, at the command of his evil father, Hiranyakashup. Another speaks of the infant Krishna refusing poisonous milk from the breast of the demon Putana. In India the festival usually lasts for three days. People gather in the street to sing and dance and to squirt each other with coloured water or daub each other with paint. In the evening, at the climax of the festival, people visit the Temple to worship before decorated statues of Krishna and his consort Radha. The worshippers will sit on the floor, singing sacred hymns and songs (Bhajans), accompanied by musicians playing traditional Indian instruments. The highlight of the worship is when a tray of lit candles is passed around the crowd. The light symbolises goodness and purity – worship of light in this way is called arti. Coins are placed on the tray as gifts to the gods. Finally, everyone receives prasad – food that is holy and has been dedicated to the gods – this consists of almonds, nuts and fruits. After worship in the temple, which basically follows the same pattern as on other occasions, the congregation goes outside to place food offerings on a huge bonfire: the food can be retrieved when cooked and eaten.

Divali is the festival of lights, taking its name from the Sanskrit word Deepavali, meaning 'a row or cluster of lights'. It marks the beginning of the religious New Year and takes place over five days in October/November. Clay lamps containing oil are lit in the home and may be floated in leaf cups along the river. Light symbolises the victory of virtue and goodness. Lakshmi, the goddess of success and fortune, blesses the homes of those who celebrate the festival. Gifts are exchanged and prayers and requests are made to Lakshmi for the year ahead. At this time there is a conscious attempt to repair relationships that have been fractured over the year.

Shrines and temples are common throughout India, and each home has a special area, decorated with an image of a god or goddess – human or animal. It is normally part of the woman's duties to tend to the family shrine by offering worship and prayer. Certain days of the month are widely regarded as being religiously significant. The most important days are Purnima (full moon) and Amavasya (new moon) on which many Hindus fast. Prayer and meditation are common practices among Hindus and there is hardly an aspect of daily life for which some god is not responsible and to whom prayer should be made.

5.4   CHALLENGES TO THE TRADITION

The independent state of India was established as a secular republic in 1948, with the deliberate intention of reconciling different religious identities. For the most part this strategy has been successful, and given the traditional tolerant spirit of Hinduism, other religious identities such as Muslim and Sikh have co-existed alongside Hinduism, even though it is the religion of the vast majority of the inhabitants. (I say for the most part because there remains a problem in rural areas if an individual chooses to convert to another religion, either Buddhism or Christianity: conversions to Islam are rare.) Over the last decade, however, increasing tensions have begun to emerge between the different religious groups, particularly between Hindus and Muslims. Animosities between these two groups go back to the origins of the state and the division of the Indian sub-continent into India and North and South

Pakistan. The adoption of a secular constitution by India was a bold attempt to defuse tension. But the rise of militant fundamentalism within Islam and political tensions within modern Pakistan has heightened distrust between Hindus and Muslims. This in turn has contributed to an alignment between nationalist politics and religion among Hindus, and has seen the emergence of unashamedly nationalist, Hindu religious parties as one of the main political forces in India. This alignment is also in part due to the perception that a secular approach to politics and social policy, of the kind favoured by successive Indian governments, has failed to reflect public support for distinctively Hindu religious and moral commitments. In other words, there is a perception that the religious and moral views of the majority of the inhabitants have not been sufficiently reflected in public policy.

This deepening alignment between Hinduism and politics also illustrates a further tension within Hinduism, that is, Hinduism's relation to modernity and the process of secularisation. The traditionalist response (as evidenced in the rise of religious political parties) is to resist the marginalisation of religion that is associated with secularisation. One can understand this reaction, in that there is accumulating evidence from the modern Western nations, where the process of secularisation is much further advanced, that a decline in the influence of religion leads to a decline both in standards of public behaviour and in participation in civic life. Religion provides purpose and direction for individuals as it integrates them into a community of believers with shared values, enthusiasms and moral commitments. The promiscuity, materialism and individualism of Western society are regarded by many Indian commentators as resulting from the disparagement of religion and therefore constitute a warning against any equivocation in the task of opposing secularisation within their own society. But what kind of Hinduism should be maintained in opposition to the forces of secularisation? A revival of traditional religion entails support for the concepts of caste and varna and a fairly constricted public role for women. Are the kinds of rigid social divisions required by the caste system consistent with justice and are such divisions of the essence of Hinduism? Questions of religious identity and religious authenticity are common to the religions as they grapple with the twin imperatives of being faithful to their roots while simultaneously being relevant to the diverse needs of individuals in the modern world.

The question of identity and religious authenticity is felt most acutely by young Hindus growing up in the West. What does being faithful to their tradition require of them as they live and work in a predominantly secular, post-Christian society? How are the laws of purity and pollution to be applied in a non-Hindu world? Whichever answer we give to these questions some attention needs to be given to the fact that religious identity is a fluid and changing notion both for individuals and for communities. Furthermore, rather than view the individual as possessing a single identity, it may be more accurate to see the individual as assuming different identities as he interacts in different contexts, for different purposes with different people. Perhaps the notion of a single identity presupposes a coherence of belief, action and emotion that many of us fail to realise or demonstrate, Hindus included.

6

Buddhism

Hold fast to the truth as a lamp. Seek salvation alone in the truth. Look not for assistance to anyone besides yourself.

The Buddha

Of the Eastern religions, Buddhism has been most successful in attracting Western followers. Its focus upon 'mindfulness' is a welcome distraction for some from the frenetic nature of modern urban life and its cultivation of a sense of the tragic resonates with those whose material needs are fully met, but whose spiritual needs remain unfulfilled. Like Christianity it has a historical founder, and like Christianity it was from the beginning a missionary religion.

An overview of Buddhism

Each new monk to the monastic community affirms his commitment to Buddhism in the following three-fold vow, referred to as the three jewels of Buddhism:

> I go to the Buddha for refuge.
> I go to the Dharma (Doctrine) for refuge.
> I go to the Sangha for refuge.

This credal affirmation will structure our overview of Buddhism, though a note will be added on the various schools of Buddhism.

The life of the Buddha

According to the Pali Tripitaka (the sacred scriptures of Theravada Buddhism) and later commentaries, Siddhartha Gautama was born in the sixth or fifth century BCE in the Sakya kingdom (in modern India), of which his parents were king and queen. The night before his birth, Siddhartha's mother, the queen Mahamaya, had a dream in which an elephant carrying a lotus flower in its trunk entered her womb through the right side of her body. Brahmins (Vedic priests), upon hearing of the dream, predicted that the child would become either a great monarch or a Buddha, 'an Enlightened one'. Soon after his birth, 108 Brahmins were invited to the name-giving ceremony. Eight of these men were experts in interpreting bodily marks. Seven of the eight predicted that if the child remained at home, he would become a great ruler, but if the child left home and travelled, he would become a Buddha. The eighth and youngest of the group, Kondanna, predicted that the child would definitely become a Buddha.

The young prince was raised in great luxury and wealth, as his father, King Suddhodana, made every effort to influence him in favour of a worldly life. But at the age of twenty-eight, as he travelled on his chariot beyond the palace walls, Siddhartha witnessed a number of scenes that spoke to him of the inherent suffering in life, then finally he saw a holy man who was rapt in meditation. Struck by the ascetic's serene appearance in the midst of such worldly suffering, Siddhartha decided to renounce his wealth and embark on the path to spiritual truth and enlightenment. That night he left his family and began his travels south, where centres of learning and spiritual discipline flourished.

Siddhartha followed the teachings and meditation practices of a number of celebrated spiritual teachers but he remained frustrated in his quest for truth. He then joined with a group of five ascetics, among whom was Kondanna, the Brahman who had predicted his future as a Buddha. For nearly six years, Siddhartha lived a life of self-denial and extreme austerity. It is recorded that for a time he survived on a single grain of rice a day. Eventually he became too weak to continue and he realised that the path of self-mortification did not lead to wisdom and spiritual insight. His companions, viewing this change of mind as a weakness, left him to seek truth alone.

A little later Siddhartha sat at the base of a pipal tree, also known as a bodhi or bo tree, and decided not to rise until he had attained enlightenment. In the first part of the night, after he defeated Mara, the Evil One, Siddhartha learned of his former existences. During the second part, he gained the power to see the passing away and rebirth of beings. In the last part of the night he came to a knowledge of the Four Noble Truths. The Scriptures record him claiming that his 'mind was emancipated.... Ignorance was dispelled, knowledge arose; darkness was dispelled, light arose'. On encountering his former ascetic companions in the Deer Park in Benares, he told them of his experience. They were struck by the change in his demeanour and believed his message. The Buddha then delivered to them his first sermon, 'Setting in Motion the Wheel of Truth'. He explained to them that one should follow neither extreme self-indulgence nor self-mortification. Instead one should follow the middle path, that is the Noble Eightfold Path. With these five new disciples, the Buddha created a community around profession of the three jewels: the Buddha, the Dharma (teachings) and the Sangha, the monastic community.

The Buddha spent the remaining forty-five years of his life preaching and teaching as he travelled on foot throughout North-Eastern India speaking to audiences of different backgrounds. The Buddha died, probably of food poisoning, at the small town of Kusinara, not far from his original homeland. His remains were cremated and are stored in a *stupa*, a bell shaped monument. According to tradition, the Buddha's last words were, 'decay is inherent in all things: be sure to strive with clarity of mind for nirvana'. Before the end of his life the question was raised as to who would be his successor and who would exercise authority in his name. In conversations with his cousin and personal attendant, Ananda, the Buddha stated that there was no need for a successor since he had never thought of himself as a leader. He instead instructed that the Dharma should be the guide after he was gone and that the monks should continue to uphold the Vinaya, the code of rules for monastic life. The Buddha believed that individuals should think for themselves on matters of doctrine and test their worth before accepting them as true. As a result of his instruction, Buddhism has never established a central body or authority that rules on right belief and doctrine. No single institution has the ability to interpret or evaluate doctrine for the religion as a whole.

The teaching of the Buddha
The essence of the teachings (Dharma) of the Buddha are contained in his first sermon. In it he expounds 'the Four Noble Truths'.

> What, O Monks, is the Noble Truth of Suffering? Birth is suffering, sickness is suffering, old age is suffering, death is suffering. Pain, grief, sorrow, lamentation, and despair are suffering. Association with that which is unpleasant is suffering, dissociation from what is pleasant is suffering. Not to get what one wants is suffering. In short, the five factors of individuality are suffering.
> This, O Monks, is the Truth of the Arising of Suffering. It is this thirst or craving (*tanha*) which gives

rise to rebirth, which is bound up with passionate delight and which seeks fresh pleasure now here and now there in the form of a thirst for sensual pleasure, a thirst for existence, and a thirst for non-existence.

This, O Monks, is the Truth of the Cessation of Suffering. It is the utter cessation of that craving (*tanha*), the withdrawal from it, the renouncing of it, the rejection of it, liberation from it, non-attachment to it.

This, O Monks, is the Truth of the Path that leads to the cessation of suffering. It is this Noble Eightfold Path, which consists of Right View, Right Resolve, Right Speech, Right Action, Right Livelihood, Right Effort, Right Mindfulness, and Right Meditation.

The First Noble Truth is the Truth of *Dukkha*, which is generally translated as 'suffering', though the term has a much wider and deeper philosophical meaning. The defining feature of existence for the Buddha is dukkha, by which he means that life is necessarily subject to anguish and pain. Old age, sickness and death are universal. Separation from loved ones and pleasant conditions, association with unpleasant persons and conditions, and not getting what one desires – these are all sources of suffering and 'unsatisfactoriness'. Dukkha encompasses the whole state of being or existence. Everything in life is subject to change.

The Buddha regarded the human person as a flux of energy comprising five aggregates: the Aggregates of Form, Feeling, Perception, Mental Formation, and Consciousness. The impermanent nature of existence will ultimately thwart the human search for stability and constancy. Nothing substantial endures. The Buddha believed that when we train our minds to observe the functioning of mental and physical processes we will come to recognise the impermanent nature of human existence. We will see how life is subject to change and as a consequence that there is no real substance or entity or Self to which we can attach an enduring identity. When we become aware of the unsatisfactory nature of life, we will naturally want to escape, and this should cause us to focus our minds on the nature of truth and salvation.

The Second Noble Truth explains the Origin or Cause of suffering. Tanha or 'craving' is the universal cause of suffering. It includes not only desire for sensual pleasures, wealth and power, but also attachment to ideas, views, opinions, concepts, and beliefs. Not realising the true nature of one's self, one clings to things that are impermanent, changeable and perishable. The failure to satisfy one's desires through things in the world causes disappointment and exacerbates suffering. Craving is a powerful mental force present in all of us. It is the root cause of our sufferings. It is this craving which binds us the wheel of rebirth (Samsara) – the repeated cycle of birth and death.

The Third Noble Truth points to the cessation of suffering. Where there is no craving, there is no becoming, no rebirth. Where there is no rebirth, there is no decay: no old age, no death, hence no suffering. Suffering is ended, once and for all. Although the Buddha's diagnosis of the human situation seems unremittingly negative, his teaching is ultimately positive, in that he professed to have found a means of escape from the human situation. Suffering can be ended once craving is overcome, and as a result Nirvana or salvation is attained. At this stage the fire of greed, hatred, and delusion are extinguished.

The Fourth Noble Truth explains the Path that leads to the cessation of suffering. It is called the Noble Eightfold Path.

Right Understanding	the acceptance of Buddhist teachings.
Right Resolve	making a serious commitment to developing right attitudes.

Right Speech	telling the truth.
Right Action	abstaining from wrongful bodily behaviour such as killing, stealing, or behaving wrongfully with respect to sensual pleasures.
Right Livelihood	not engaging in an occupation that causes harm to others.
Right Effort	gaining control of one's thoughts and cultivating positive states of mind.
Right Mindfulness	cultivating constant awareness.
Right Meditation	developing deep levels of mental calm through various techniques that concentrate the mind and integrate the personality.

The eightfold path is normally divided into three parts, wisdom (understanding and resolve), morality (speech, action and livelihood) and concentration (effort, mindfulness and meditation). Morality is the avoidance of evil or unwholesome actions, say actions that are tainted by greed, hatred and delusion, and the performance of good or wholesome actions, that is, actions that are free from greed, hatred and delusion, and motivated by liberality, loving-kindness and wisdom. The purpose of good conduct and moral restraint is to free one's mind from remorse. The mind that is free from remorse is naturally calm and tranquil, and ready for concentration with awareness. The concentrated and cultured mind is a contemplative and analytical mind. It is capable of seeing cause and effect, and the true nature of existence, thus paving the way for wisdom and spiritual insight. Wisdom in the Buddhist context is the realisation of the validity of the Four Noble Truths and the resolve to follow its injunctions.

The Sangha

The Sangha is the assembly of Buddhist monks that studies, transmits and preserves the teachings of Buddhism. Given the relevance of the Sangha to our later discussion of 'The Community of Believers' we will postpone further comment until then.

Schools of Buddhism

The first major division in Buddhism was a result of the First Buddhist Council held in 483 BCE. This Council was called in response to the question of the direction Buddhism should take following the death of its founder. The decision was made at the Council that Buddhism should be chiefly a monastic religion, since only through membership of the monastic order was it realistically possible to achieve enlightenment. This decision led to turmoil and a split within Buddhism, from which Hinayana and Mahayana Buddhism (also sometimes referred to as Northern, Sanskrit or Indian Buddhism) arose. (A third major vehicle, Vajrayana or Tantric Buddhism, is sometimes distinguished from Hinayana and Mahayana. It shares much with the latter and for this reason we will not consider it further.)

Hinayana / Theravada

Hinayana, 'Lesser Vehicle', is concerned more with the individual than society as a whole. From the Hinayana division the only surviving school is the Theravada, 'Teachings of the Elders', which spread south and east of India into present day Sri Lanka, Southeast Asia and Bangladesh. Followers of this school trace their tradition back to the senior monks of the first Sangha and rely on the Pali canon as their source of scriptures. The goal of Theravada Buddhists is to become an Arhant, the 'accomplished ascetic who attains nirvana through self-effort'. Although women and men are able to become arhants, its achievement requires the kind of dedication and discipline available only through membership of the Sangha.

Mahayana

Mahayana means 'Great Vehicle', in the sense of 'great vehicle across the ocean of suffering'. The division between Hinayana and Mahayana came to centre on the proper interpretation of the Buddha's life and teaching. In the earliest Buddhist sources the Buddha is presented as a human being who propounded a radical system of self-discipline leading to salvation. The achievement of salvation is by self-effort. The Buddhists who founded the Mahayana school disputed the completeness of the earliest sources and contended that the Buddha made provision for prayer and for the transfer of merit from one individual to another. For them Buddhism is a religion of grace and worship. In contrast to the Theravada ideal of the arhant, followers of the Mahayana tradition strive to become Bodhisattvas. A bodhisattva, 'enlightenment hero' is one who has taken a vow to reach Buddhahood, but foregoes entrance into nirvana so that he may remain in this world as long as there are creatures to be saved. Salvation is open to all and can be attained by both men and women, monks and laity. Motivated by compassion and selfless love, the Bodhisattva helps the unenlightened 'by example, by reducing their sufferings in practical ways, by encouraging and helping them, and by teaching them the path to liberation'. Mahayanists believe that the merit accrued by the bodhisattva's deferral of nirvana can be transferred to others, who may gain salvation as a result. The bodhisattva's willingness and desire to help others is proof of his true compassion and his freedom from desire.

6.1   A VISION OF SALVATION

The achievement of salvation is central to Buddhism, both in its Theravada and its Mahayana forms. Of course, as with Hinduism, this does not mean that every Buddhist is actively striving to achieve liberation in his or her current lifetime. For many the proximate goal of a better rebirth is the focus of their commitment to Buddhism. Perhaps after faithful commitment and successive rebirths one will become a member of the Sangha and so increase the chance of finally achieving liberation. From the perspective of this current rebirth, the ultimate goal of salvation is a distant reality for most Buddhists, albeit a distant reality whose influence shapes their daily pattern of life and existence.

Like Hinduism, Buddhism regards salvation as the overcoming of karma-samsara. Karma refers to the effects that follow from human choice. All choices have effects, either good or bad. Sometimes choices have an effect on others, such as helping or robbing someone and sometimes they affect only the agent. Through our decisions we shape our character and future. This can be summed up in the proverb, 'sow an act, reap a habit; sow a habit, reap a character; sow a character, reap a destiny'. Every act bears fruit and this binds us to the wheel of life. The actions performed in one life initiate another life and so on. The cycle of rebirth is called Samsara. The cycle can continue for eternity and will end only when the person attains salvation (nirvana). There are as many as six realms (early sources list five, but six are mentioned in later works) into which one may be reborn. On the upper half are the realms of the gods, titans and humans, while ghosts, animals and hell are on the bottom. Rebirth as a human is considered very desirable and difficult to reach. While there are higher levels of rebirth, human existence has the greatest potential for spiritual progress and offers the best chance of escaping cyclic existence. Being reborn as a god, one may lose sight of the need for release. Leading a human existence, by contrast, provides constant reminders of the need for salvation and allows one to learn and teach the Dharma. The school of Theravada gives an unusual twist to the doctrine of karma-samsara, in that it denies that there is an eternal soul that is passed on throughout successive rebirths. The Buddha's radical doctrine of the impermanence of all things is believed to entail that there is no permanent self or soul (*anatta*), the self is a bundle of constantly changing 'aggregates' or energies: at rebirth it is the aggregates that continue in a new earthly form. By contract many Mahayana Buddhists, in common with Hindus, accept the existence of a substantial self or soul that endures over the generations.

The Buddhist equivalent of the English term salvation is Nirvana, it is formed of *Ni* and *Vana*. *Ni* is a negative particle and *vana* means 'lusting or craving', literally nirvana is 'the end of desire and craving'. Some writers translate the word nirvana into English as 'non-attachment', in that craving is extinguished and no desire remains. A pure state of non-attachment means that salvation is achieved and the cycle of rebirth is broken. One escapes from the realm of suffering and pain. The Buddha likened nirvana to the extinguishing of a flame. This should not be interpreted to mean that nirvana is a state of nothingness or annihilation. The reality of nirvana, according to Theravada, transcends human language, in that words are incapable of capturing and expressing its fullness. Much of the Buddha's language was evocative and paradoxical as he attempted to put into speech what he believed defied linguistic expression. Language points us in the right direction but it does not literally describe spiritual experience. Mahayana Buddhism interprets nirvana much more colourfully, for example as 'a land of bliss' and 'a heavenly realm'. One central interpretation is that of nirvana as mystical identity with the One Supreme Spirit. Such interpretations (reflecting Hindu influence) seem inconsistent with the earliest recorded teaching of the Buddha, but then the Mahayanists question the completeness of the sources that claim to represent the Buddha's original teaching. They supplement the earliest written Pali scriptures with additional Sanskrit scriptures.

Nirvana is attained by adherence to the Four Noble Truths and practice of the Noble Eightfold Path. We have already outlined Buddhist teaching on these themes. At this stage in our discussion it is worth noting that Theravada Buddhism does not look to a saviour god in the quest for liberation. Ironically, for the Buddha, even the gods are bound to the wheel of rebirth. They too are subject to anguish and suffering, though to a lesser degree than humans. In this sense their situation is worse than the human situation, for the muted truth of suffering is more easily ignored by them and the gravity of their conditioned existence is not appreciated. Theravada Buddhism has been described as 'a radical system of self-deliverance'. The Buddha does not intercede on our behalf or bestow grace and favour upon his followers. Each individual must follow the path of morality, concentration and wisdom for himself. Indeed so strenuous are the demands of the Eightfold Path that many Theravada Buddhists believe that only those who join the monastic community of the Sangha have any realistic chance of achieving nirvana. T.H. Huxley has described Theravada Buddhism as 'a system which knows no God in the Western sense, which denies a soul to man, which counts the belief in immortality a blunder, which refuses any efficacy to prayer and sacrifice, which bids men to look to nothing but their own efforts for salvation, which in its original purity knew nothing of vows of obedience and never sought the aid of the secular arm: yet spread over a considerable portion of the world with marvellous rapidity – and is still the dominant creed of a large fraction of mankind'.

Mahayana schools offer the prospect of nirvana to all. The numerous Buddhas and Bodhisattvas are committed to boundless love. They act to save their followers from the torments of hell. Their followers in turn worship and serve them by acts of dedication and by supporting their temples and the priests who attend the sacred images and perform sacred rituals. Different geographical areas look to different Buddhas and Bodhisattvas for grace and favour. There has been much discussion by western scholars of Pure Land Buddhism with its focus upon Amitabha Buddha, 'the Buddha of Infinite Light'. Some find in this school similarities with Protestant

Christianity. Amitabha claims that he will save all those who turn to him in faith.

6.2   THE COMMUNITY OF BELIEVERS

The Sangha is the community or assembly of Buddhist monks. It serves to preserve and practise the teachings of the Buddha. The Sangha serves the laity through example and the teaching of morality: in supporting the Sangha the laity acquires merit, which in turn contributes to a better rebirth. The Buddha instituted the Sangha and gathered around himself a group of faithful disciples to whom he acted as spiritual guide and director. At first all monks were ordained by the Buddha, but as members increased this proved an impossible task, so senior monks were also authorised to confer ordination. The main aim of the Sangha is to provide a context for the practice of Buddhism. Nirvana is possible for all, irrespective of caste, if there is faithful adherence to the teachings of the Buddha; the Sangha provides the indispensable context for faithful adherence.

The Sangha is divided into separate but parallel religious orders for men and women. A further distinction is made between novices and those who have undergone a further ordination. Technically the term monk is reserved for this latter category, that is, those who commit themselves to the Sangha for life. Many young men enter the Sangha for a short period before adulthood and marriage in order to achieve merit and develop a spiritual discipline for later life. A novice, whether male of female, is expected to observe the Ten Precepts (the first five of which are also enjoined on the laity): they are all negative prohibitions – not to kill, steal, commit sexual misconduct, utter falsehood, consume intoxicants or drugs – not to eat certain foods, dance, use perfumes or adornments, live in luxury or possess money. A monk after higher ordination is expected to observe over two hundred additional rules, many of which are believed to go back to the life and example of the Buddha.

Originally, Buddhist monks lived a mendicant life of poverty and strict sexual abstinence. They were only allowed to own three robes, one girdle, an alms bowl, a razor, a needle, and a water strainer to be used to filter insects from the drinking water. During the rainy season they came together for reflection and teaching. Within a few centuries of the Buddha's death, however, some of the monks began to establish permanent monastic settlements (*Viharas*). Gradually a division of labour and hierarchical structure emerged in the monasteries, with the abbot as the head of the community. Seniority is ideally based upon commitment and maturity with regard to spiritual discernment and experience. Most monasteries are independent and there is no centralised authority in Buddhism. Although there is variation between the different schools of Buddhism, most of the standards on poverty, begging and sexual abstinence have been loosened. Begging has generally become a mere symbolic gesture of humility. The growth of large monasteries has led to a relaxation of the rules of poverty, and in some schools sexual intercourse is allowed.

All members of the community come together for collective activities such as confession ceremonies and regular recitation of the monastic code. The majority of monks are heavily involved in the religious life of the laity. Members of the community serve as ritual specialists and officiate at various ceremonies. They give sermons, chant texts, and participate in offerings and other merit making rituals. Other monks will devote themselves more fully to the cultivation of their own spiritual life, spending long hours in meditation.

Authority resides in the teachings of the Buddha and in the rules that regulate the religious life. Buddhists speak of the authority of experience and not the authority of position. Each person has to authenticate the truth of the Buddha's way for

himself or herself. Obedience is to the truth. Each must decide
which path to choose. It is not uncommon for Buddhists to
characterise the monotheistic religions as dogmatic and
authoritarian and to contrast them with the democratic and
experiential nature of Buddhism.

6.3   A CELEBRATING TRADITION

There are many special or holy days held throughout the year
by Buddhist communities. Many of these days celebrate the
birthdays of Bodhisattvas in the Mahayana tradition or other
significant dates in the Buddhist calendar. On a festival day, lay
people will typically go the local temple or monastery and offer
food to the monks and listen to a talk about the Dharma. In the
afternoon, they distribute food to the poor to gain merit and in
the evening join in a ceremony of circumambulation around a
stupa three times as a sign of respect to the Buddha, his
Dhamma and the Sangha. The day will conclude with
meditation and chanting of portions of the sacred scriptures.
      Some holy days are specific to a particular Buddhist
tradition or ethnic group. There are two aspects to take into
consideration regarding Buddhist festivals. First, most
Buddhists, with the exception of the Japanese, use the Lunar
Calendar, and second, the dates of Buddhist festivals vary from
country to country and between Buddhist traditions. We will
focus on two major festivals, Vesak or Buddha's Day, which is
celebrated by most Buddhists, and Poson, which is celebrated in
Sri Lanka.
      Traditionally, the Buddha's Birthday is known as Vesak (the
month of his birth in the Indian calender) or Visakah Puja
(Buddha's Birthday Celebrations). It celebrates the birth,
enlightenment and death of the Buddha on the first full moon
day in May, except in a leap year when the festival is held in
June. The theme of the Buddha's enlightenment predominates
and accordingly in Buddhist homes and temples lights are lit

and decorations put up. There are symbols of illumination everywhere and Buddhists gather before images of the Buddha to make offerings: gifts of food and money will also be made to Buddhist priests. Many will attend the temples and monasteries to hear sermons on the Buddha's life and enlightenment. Stress is placed upon the Buddha's kindness and love and his role as a model for all to follow. Caged birds are released and special gifts are given to the poor. People vow to follow the teachings of the Buddha for another year and there is a sense of community and personal renewal. Nowadays many send greetings cards illustrated with scenes from the life of the Buddha.

The festival of Poson in Theravada Buddhism, Sri Lanka, commemorates the coming of Buddhism to the island (in 250 BCE). The Indian Emperor Ashoka was keen to spread the teachings of the Buddha and he sent his son, a monk, Mahinda, to convert the inhabitants. Some temples, especially in towns, organise religious processions in which an image of Mahinda, usually made of cardboard, looking like an idealised Buddhist monk and on top of a cart, is paraded through the streets to dancing and the sound of drums and music. Large numbers of people take part in the procession. At the end there is a great display of fireworks.

There is a simple ceremony in Theravada Buddhism to celebrate the birth of a child. The parents take the child to the local temple to be named. A monk sprinkles the child with water and pronounces a blessing. A wax candle is burned and the molten wax allowed to fall into a bowl of pure water. This symbolises the union of the four elements – air, fire, wind and water. The union of the elements is a symbol of the harmony that the child will achieve with all of life and nature when he or she grows to adulthood. At a later stage, it is customary for young men to leave home for a time and retire to a monastery before embarking on adult life. This allows time for meditation and reflection before the duties of adulthood are undertaken. It also is a means of accumulating merit so that one will find favour in later enterprises. Some will stay on and join the Sangha for life.

Marriage is also an event that is marked by religious rituals and endowed with religious meaning. Marriages in Buddhism may take place either in the bride's home or in the temple. If at home, a shrine will be specially erected, complete with a Buddha image, candles and flowers. The couple and assembly should recite or chant some passages from the Buddhist Scriptures. Following this, the couple should light the candles and incense sticks, and offer flowers, placing them on and around the table on which the image of the Buddha stands. The bride and groom should then, in turn, recite the traditional commitments expected of them in the Buddhist tradition. 'Towards my wife I undertake to love and respect her, be kind and considerate, be faithful, delegate domestic management, provide gifts to please her', is said by the groom, to which the bride responds, 'Towards my husband I undertake to perform my household duties efficiently, be hospitable to my in-laws and friends of my husband, be faithful, protect and invest our earnings, discharge my responsibilities lovingly and conscientiously.' Finally, the assembly should recite a further passage from the scriptures as a blessing.

Funeral rites are the most elaborate of all the life-cycle ceremonies and the rites entered into most fully by the monks. The people rely upon monks to chant the verses that will benefit the deceased and to conduct all funeral rites and memorial services. To conduct the rites for the dead may be considered the one indispensable service rendered by the monks to the community. Theravada Buddhists follow the Indian custom of burning the body at death. The Buddha's body was cremated and this set the example for many Buddhists, even in the West. According to tradition, when a person is dying an effort should be made to fix his mind upon the Buddhist Scriptures or to get him to repeat one of the names of the Buddha. Sometimes four syllables representing sacred words are written on a piece of paper and put in the mouth of the dying. It is hoped that if the last thoughts of the patient are directed to the precepts of Buddhism, then the fruit of this meritorious act will benefit the deceased in his or her new existence. After death a bathing ceremony takes place in which relatives and friends pour water over one hand of the deceased. The body is then placed in a coffin and surrounded with wreaths, candles and sticks of incense. If possible a photograph of the deceased is placed alongside, and coloured lights are suspended about the coffin. Sometimes the cremation is deferred for a week to allow distant relatives to attend or to show special honour to the dead. In this case a chapter of monks comes to the house one or more times each day to chant from the Abhidharma, one of the most sacred writings of Buddhism. Food is offered to the officiating monks as part of the merit-making for the deceased. The food offered in the name of the dead is known as *Matakabhatta* from *mataka* ('one who is dead'). As long as the body is present the spirit can benefit from the gifts presented, the sermons preached and the chants uttered before it. When the body is cremated the spirit is cut off from the world; it is best therefore not to force the spirit to enter the next world finally and irrevocably until it has had the benefit of a number of religious services designed to improve its status.

6.4   CHALLENGES TO THE TRADITION

The individualistic nature of Buddhism is attractive to many in the West. Its great variety of forms and expressions are suggestive of a religious path that can be tailored to individual needs. For some, Theravada's agnosticism about the nature of the divine and its refusal to speculate on metaphysical matters offer a welcome contrast to the monotheistic religions where definition and orthodoxy have traditionally been central concerns. Equally, Theravada's emphasis upon the self (in the sense of overcoming the self) fits in well with the individualistic nature of modern Western life. Meditation and religious exercises bring an element of calm and stability to lives otherwise assailed by rapidly changing patterns of work and increasingly complex webs of personal and professional relationships. But critical questions also intrude, for in the attempt to make Buddhism attractive to the West much of its original ascetic orientation has been abandoned. The teaching of Buddhism is often tailored to fit an audience more concerned with achieving balance and contentment in life than with renouncing all to achieve nirvana. What is Buddhism without the strict ethic that was central to its original formulation? By contrast how can a proper monastic life-style be maintained in our modern pluralist, post-Christian societies by those Westerners who seek to be faithful to the Buddha's Dharma? Can there be a faithful community of monks where there is no wider lay community to support and encourage?

The orientation of Buddhism towards nirvana and the accompanying disparagement of involvement in the mundane things of life have meant that a strong tradition of social thought or social ethics has not developed. Involvement with the world binds us to the wheel of rebirth and social improvements may only disguise the all-pervasive nature of suffering that characterises existence. This otherworldly orientation, coupled with the depreciation of lay religion, in that religious earnestness requires membership of the Sangha, has meant that Buddhism has struggled to retain relevance to the social and political realities that confront contemporary Buddhists in South-East Asia. Those Buddhists who aspire to social justice and a new ethical order for society have had difficulty finding intellectual resources to support their liberal commitments. There have been some provocative attempts to combine Buddhism with Marxist philosophy in order to overcome what some see as a lacuna in traditional Buddhist thought. Such concerns of course are far removed from the form of Buddhism that is typically offered and practised in the West. In this context basic liberties and an abundance of material goods are assumed; Buddhism is affirmed as a means of curbing the acquisitive self and of restraining the worse excesses of material consumption and a licentious lifestyle. Such matters are far removed from the preoccupations of those who practise the way of the Buddha in South-East Asia and the Far East.

7

Inter-Faith Dialogue

Dialogue is typically defined as 'a conversation between two or more people involving an exchange of ideas and opinions.' At one level each of us engages in dialogue every day as we discuss and converse with others. At a deeper level we might want to reserve the term dialogue for those occasions where there is a genuine respect each for each and where there is real and reflective engagement between the different parties to dialogue. Inter-faith dialogue, as the name implies, describes conversations between adherents of different religions (inter-faith dialogue and inter-religious dialogue are synonymous terms). Dialogue carries connotations of engagement and personal encounter. At a theological level one may enter into dialogue with other religions by reading about their beliefs and values, but this seems to reflect an impoverished notion of dialogue that omits the element of personal experience and conversation. Certainly much Christian theological reflection on other faiths in the past was pursued either without any real personal contact with adherents of other religions or, where there was contact, without any real listening to what the other person had to say. One of the reasons of course for a lack of dialogue in the past was that cultures and religions were relatively isolated from each other. In addition, religions were

aligned so closely with particular cultures that the self-critical
element that is essential to genuine dialogue was missing. Each
person was so assured of the truth of his own position that
there was presumed to be no need to listen attentively to
others. The 'other' was to be evangelised and not engaged in
dialogue. There was a sense in which dialogue was only
assumed to be relevant when there was a meeting of cultural
equals, and given Western 'Christian' colonial dominance, the
notion of serious dialogue with adherents of non-Christian
faiths was not countenanced. This is an exaggeration of course.
But it is interesting to note how genuine efforts to understand
and appreciate both the *strengths* and weakness of other faiths
were often produced in cultural contexts where Christianity
could not rely upon force of arms and had to engage
respectfully with those with whom it differed.

Types of dialogue
We have focused on the notion of inter-faith dialogue as
personal encounters between adherents of different faiths, but
dialogue can mean different things to different people. Eric
Sharpe, a distinguisher scholar of religion has identified four
different interpretations or types of inter-faith dialogue. He
distinguished between discursive dialogue, human dialogue,
secular dialogue and interior dialogue. The aim of discursive
dialogue is to understand and appreciate the religious beliefs of
others. We could also think of discursive dialogue as
intellectual dialogue, though use of the term intellectual
should not be interpreted to exclude the relevance of such
attitudes as respect, sincerity and honesty. In discursive dialogue
one learns about other religions through interaction and
conversation with those who believe and practise them. What
was read or recounted second hand becomes alive through
personal contact. Mention of personal contact conveniently
leads into the category of human dialogue. The notion behind
this kind of dialogue is that if there is to be a true meeting of

minds between people of different faiths they need to move beyond the aim of acquiring knowledge about each other and meet each other as authentic human beings. Persons encounter other persons and in this exchange there can emerge a deep sense of our common identity as humans, an identity that is stronger than the religious doctrines that divide. According to Sharpe, secular dialogue, the third type of dialogue, is a form of dialogue where individuals of different religious persuasions come together to cooperate in joint social and political programmes to ameliorate the human situation. Welfare programmes and joint support for initiatives to challenge injustice and human rights abuses would be examples of secular dialogue. The fourth type of inter-faith dialogue to which Sharpe refers is interior dialogue. This form of dialogue centres on prayer and meditation. Inspiration is drawn from mysticism and contemplative forms of spirituality. The aim is to penetrate beyond differences of belief and experience the divine reality that lies at the heart of all genuine religion. Such a form of dialogue, it is suggested, is particularly appropriate for Christians engaging in dialogue with Hindus and Buddhists. Mystical experience provides a point of convergence for all three religions. The language and spirituality of the respective mystical traditions offers the hope of reconciliation between them.

Sharpe's classification and review of different types of dialogue clearly reflect theological influences that were prominent at the time of his writing in 1974. This is particularly apparent in his discussion of human dialogue. Much of the inspiration for this form of dialogue came from the writings of the Jewish theologian and philosopher, Martin Buber (1878-1965). According to Buber our ordinary human relations with each other can become an occasion for an encounter with the absolute other, the 'eternal Thou'. In a truly human encounter, characterised by reciprocity and openness, there is always the possibility of a divine encounter as the 'eternal Thou' reveals himself in and through authentic human relationships. Those influenced by Buber's thought conceived of religious dialogue as a means of occasioning an existential encounter with the divine. Religious authenticity is realised in an encounter of faith as ordinary human relationships become a vehicle for a uniquely person manifestation of God. We need not spend time considering the plausibility of this particular existentialist interpretation of religious dialogue, suffice to say that such an interpretation is now only of historical interest. Yet the strangely dated feel of Sharpe's discussion of the category of human dialogue alerts us to an important and general point about the nature of some interpretations of inter-religious dialogue, namely that they are conditioned by theological and religious commitments. If inter-faith dialogue is confined to the activity of meeting adherents of other religions and learning about their faith, as in discursive dialogue, then noting crucial to a theological interpretation of other faiths is implied. Of course, the natural next step is to reflect on the implications of such an encounter on one's own interpretation of the relationship between Christianity and other religions. But in an important sense participation in discursive inter-faith dialogue does not commit one to or presuppose any particular theological stance on Christianity's relationship to other religions. This is clearly not the case with regard to human dialogue or interior dialogue. According to both these types of inter-faith dialogue, doctrines and beliefs are secondary to authentic religious experience which is presumed to lie at the heart of the different religions. One can appreciate how dialogue along such lines can be developed. The Christian might assert that in mysticism there is a genuine experience of union with the divine but that the Christian interpretation of the divine is to be preferred to that of other religions; or it might be asserted that the different religions witness to the rich and mysterious nature of the divine, and so on.

The point of noting the theological assumptions and implications of certain types of inter-faith dialogue is not to commend or criticise but simply to record the fact that inter-faith dialogue is often conditioned by theological commitments. In a sense inter-faith dialogue naturally raises the question of Christianity's relation to other religions, either as a consequence of dialogue, as in discursive dialogue, or as a precursor to dialogue, where both human and interior dialogue presuppose a particular theological interpretation of Christianity in relation to other faiths. But perhaps to think of Christianity's proper theological attitude to other religions as either presupposed before dialogue or consequent upon dialogue is to falsify the nature of dialogue, for it is precisely as one is engaged in dialogue that one's attitudes and preconceptions are challenged and changed. The testimony of many who engage in inter-faith dialogue is that through dialogue they arrive at a different conclusion from which they started. Dialogue challenges received opinions and inherited prejudices. In other words, it is through the process of meeting and reflecting upon the religious testimony and witness of others that we clarify to ourselves what we believe as followers of our own religion, and as a consequence formulate our interpretation of the relationship between the great spiritual traditions of humankind. We have already noted that the cultural superiority enjoyed by Christians and the Church for many centuries tended to mean that the beliefs and values of other religions were not taken with the seriousness that they deserved, and it was only in the twentieth century with the collapse of Western colonialism and the rise of secularisation that the context was created for a more appreciative and self-critical assessment of other religions by Christians. It is to this assessment that we now turn.

The origins and development of inter-faith dialogue
The modern origins of inter-faith dialogue are usually traced to the emergence of the ecumenical movement among the Protestant Churches in the early decades of the twentieth

century and the creation of the World Council of Churches in 1948. One of the streams that eventually converged with others in the World Council of Churches was the International Missionary Council. Under its aegis a number of international conferences were organised to encourage cooperation between the various Protestant missionary bodies and to stimulate fresh thinking on issues pertinent to missionary activity. One of the effects of the first World war, coupled with a resurgence among the main world religions, no doubt bolstered by emerging nationalist movement, was to erode Western notions of superiority, and it was only a matter of time before Christian claims to religious superiority began to be challenged as well. At the Jerusalem Conference of 1928 the American W. E. Hocking argued the case for an imaginative alliance with non-Christian religions, and in subsequent publications he advocated that the religions should come together to communicate the highest spiritual values to others. Such ideas were relatively novel and the following decade the Conference at Tambaram in India (1938), under the influence of Hendrik Kraemer's *The Christian Message in a Non-Christian World*, which he wrote at the request of the organisers, asserted the traditional Christian view that the religions, however enlightened in certain respects, did not convey the grace of God, which was only to be found in Christ and his church. This position endured in the early years of the World Council of Churches, but it began to be challenged in the late 1960s by a number of prominent churchmen and ecumenical theologians. Ironically, more liberal approaches to people of other faiths were pursued by the WCC under the title of 'dialogue'. In fact in the hands of such writers as Stanley Samartha dialogue was employed as the name for a Christian approach to other religions that recognised their role in the economy of God's salvation and that urged the religions to work together for the betterment of humanity. Samartha conceived the different religions as different paths to God, each religion having its own integrity and spirituality. This view may not currently claim the allegiance of all the Churches represented in the WCC, but it does represent the view of some. At a theological and church level, however, the influence of the WCC has steadily declined since the 1970s. The house church movement, the rise of charismatic Christianity and a general move within the Protestant Churches from conceiving Church unity in institutional terms to a more spiritual conception of unity has meant that the WCC is regarded in many quarters as irrelevant to the mission and witness of the Church.

Throughout the first half of the twentieth century, for the most part, the Roman Catholic Church remained aloof from the kind of theological questions that the Protestant Churches were increasingly asking about Christianity's relations to other faiths, but it was only a matter of time before it too, under the same influences, began to engage more closely with adherents of other religions and to listen more attentively to what they had to say. An important indication of the Church's new sensitivity to adherents of non-Christian religions was evidenced by Vatican II's *Declaration of the Relation of the Church to Non-Christian Religions* (1965). The document (entitled *Nostra Aetate* in Latin) begins with the words, 'In this age of ours, when men are drawing more closely together, and the bonds of friendship between different peoples are being strengthened, the Church examines with greater care the relation she has to non-Christian religions. While affirming that the fullness of truth is contained in the Gospel of Christ as conveyed in the Church the document also acknowledges that 'The Catholic Church rejects nothing of what is true and holy in … [other] religions. She has a high regard for the manner of life and conduct, the precepts and teachings, which, although differing in many ways from her own teaching, nonetheless often reflect a ray of that truth which enlightens all men.' The declaration highlights 'the spiritual and moral goods' to be found in Hinduism, Buddhism, Islam, Judaism and other religions.

There is an extended discussion of the Church's relation to the Jews in which they are described as possessing 'a common spiritual heritage' with Christians. Persecution is condemned, a significant comment indeed given the centuries of persecution that the Jews had suffered at the hands of Christian rulers who were encouraged in their efforts by the Church. Prior to the proclamation of *Nostra Aetate*, a Secretariat for non-Christians was created in Rome in order to underline the Council's commitment to working with 'all those of good will'; in July 1988 its name was changed to the Council for Inter-Religious Dialogue.

The prominence given to relations with non-Christian faiths at Vatican II (what Eugene Hillman has called 'the wider ecumenism') has naturally resulted in increased theological interest and writing. Particularly influential has been the Jesuit theologian Karl Rahner's notion of the 'anonymous' Christian. The term refers to a non-Christian who gains salvation through faith, hope and love by the grace of Christ, mediated however imperfectly through his or her own religion, which thereby points towards its historical fulfilment in Christ and the Church. There is no salvation outside God's Church, but there are those who are members of the Church in other religions who have yet to acknowledge their inclusion in it. For some other Catholic theologians, such as Raymundo Panikkar and Paul Knitter, such 'accommodations' do not go nearly far enough. In their view the different religions should be acknowledged as historically particular but genuine vehicles of God's grace to humankind. This is undoubtedly a bold and controversial suggestion. The chief theological difficulty is that in order to effect a shift of this magnitude in the Church's traditional interpretation of non-Christian religions as not participating in the 'fullness of truth', a corresponding reinterpretation of the significance attached to Christ is needed. If the Church is correct to affirm that Jesus was God in the flesh and that his death as a ransom for sin created the conditions for reconciliation between God and humankind, it is difficult to see how religions that reject these affirmations can somehow mediate salvation. This seems to be the view and the line of argument endorsed recently by Cardinal Ratzinger, Prefect of the Congregation for the Doctrine of the Faith, in the document *Dominus Iesus* (2000). On this interpretation dialogue is compatible with evangelisation.

Religion and conflict

In this section we will look more closely at two conflict situations in the world that are commonly cited as *religious* conflicts and attempt to ascertain the precise role that religion plays in causing and sustaining each. At first blush both conflict situations are clearly religious, and this for a straightforward reason, in that people on opposing sides of both conflicts are distinguished by their religious allegiances. In Northern Ireland the distinction is between Catholics and Protestants, and in the Middle East the distinction is between Muslims and Jews. There are alternative descriptions that also fit the situations, for example Nationalists against Unionists in Northern Ireland and Palestinians against Israelis in the Middle East, and this of course immediately alerts us to the fact that there are other factors at work alongside the religious factor. The question remains, however, is religion the chief factor provoking division and civil strife?

Israel and the Palestinians

We will begin by providing a brief overview of the historical relationship between the Jews and the Palestinians in order to set in context our enquiry into the role religion plays in conflict situations.

The archaeological record indicates that the Jewish people evolved out of native Canaanite peoples and invading tribes. Some time between about 1800 and 1500 BCE, a Semitic people called Hebrews (*hapiru*) left Mesopotamia and settled in

Canaan. According to the Bible, Moses led the Israelites out of
Egypt. Under Joshua, they conquered the tribes and city states
of Canaan. Based on biblical traditions, it is estimated that
King David conquered Jerusalem about 1000 BCE and
established an Israelite kingdom over much of Canaan
including parts of Trans-Jordan. The kingdom was divided into
Judea in the south and Israel in the north following the death
of David's son, Solomon. Jerusalem remained the political and
religious centre whenever the Jews exercised sovereignty over
the country in the subsequent period, up to the Jewish revolt
in 133 CE. In 135 CE, the Romans drove the Jews out of
Jerusalem. The Romans named the area *Palaestina*, at about
this time. The name 'Palaestina', which became Palestine in
English, is derived from Herodotus, who used the term
Palaistine Syria to refer to the entire southern part of Syria,
meaning 'Philistine Syria.' Most of the Jews who continued to
practise their religion fled or were forcibly exiled from
Palestine. Jewish communities, however, continued to exist in
Galilee, the northernmost part of Palestine. Palestine was
governed by the Roman Empire until the third century CE and
then by the Byzantine Empire. In time, Christianity spread to
most of Palestine. The population consisted of Jewish converts
to Christianity or paganism, people who came with the
Romans, and others who had probably inhabited Palestine for
generations. During the sixth century, Muslim Arab armies
moved north from Arabia to conquer most of the Middle East,
including Palestine. Muslim powers controlled the region until
the early 1900s. The rulers allowed Christians and Jews to
practise their religion, though most of the local population
gradually accepted Islam and the Arab-Islamic culture of their
rulers. Jerusalem became holy to Muslims as the site where,
according to the Qur'an, Muhammad ascended to heaven after
a miraculous overnight ride on his horse, Al-Buraq. The al-
Aqsa mosque was built on the site generally regarded as the
area of the Jewish temple.

In the nineteenth century, the emancipation of Jews in Europe encouraged the blending of modern nationalistic ideas with traditional Jewish ideas about Israel and Zionism. The Zionist movement became a formal organization in 1897 with the first Zionist congress in Basle, organised by Theodore Herzl. The Zionists wished to establish a 'Jewish Homeland' in Palestine. The Zionists established farm communities in Palestine at Petah Tikva, Zichron Jacob, Rishon Letzion and elsewhere. Later they established the new city of Tel Aviv, north of Jaffa. At the same time, Palestine's Arab population grew rapidly. By 1914, the population of Palestine stood at six hundred and fifteen thousand Arabs and between eighty-five to one hundred thousand Jews.

During World War I (1914–18), the Turkish Ottoman Empire joined Germany and Austria-Hungary against the Allies. During the war Britain and its Allies courted military support from both the Arabs throughout the Middle East and the Jews in Palestine. Promises of independence were made to both groups in anticipation of the future division of the Turkish Ottoman Empire. The Balfour Declaration of 1917 stated Britain's support for the creation of a Jewish national home in Palestine, with the proviso that the civil and religious rights of the existing non-Jewish communities should not be violated. The Arabs later claimed that Palestine was included in the area promised to them, but the British denied this. In 1920, Britain received a provisional mandate from the League of Nations over Palestine, which would extend west and east of the River Jordan. The mandate, based on the Balfour declaration, was formalised in 1922. The British were to help the Jews build a national home and promote the creation of self-governing institutions. The boundary of Palestine would be limited to the area west of the river; the area east of the river, called Trans-Jordan, was made a separate British mandate. The British hoped to establish self-governing institutions in Palestine, as required by the mandate. The Arabs, however, would not accept any proposals for such institutions if they included Jews, and so no institutions were created. Subsequent attempts to resolve the differences and the setting up of independent Jewish and Arab states in Palestine failed. After the Second World War, during which about six million Jews were killed by the Nazis, there was strong support among the international community for the creation of a Jewish homeland to which many of the surviving Jews across Europe could emigrate. Jews began to return to Palestine, despite British restrictions, and the Arabs became more violent in their opposition. As the violence between Arabs and Jews escalated, so Britain found itself in the middle, subject to attack by both sides. The British found Palestine to be ungovernable and returned the mandate to the United Nations, successor to the League of Nations.

The United Nations Special Commission on Palestine recommended that Palestine be divided into an Arab state and a Jewish state. The commission called for Jerusalem to be put under international administration. The Jews accepted the UN decision, but the Arabs rejected it. The resolution divided the land into two approximately equal portions with 'irregular' borders that attempted to take account of concentrations of Palestinian and Jewish population. It soon became evident that the scheme could not work. Mutual antagonism would make it impossible for either community to tolerate the other. The Arab League (a group of surrounding Arab nations) declared a war to rid Palestine of the Jews. The British could do little to stop the fighting. On May 14, 1948, the Jews proclaimed the independent State of Israel, and the British withdrew from Palestine. The next day, neighbouring Arab nations attacked Israel. The fighting was conducted in several brief periods, punctuated by ceasefire agreements. The Arabs and Palestinians lost their initial advantage when they failed to organise and unite. When the fighting ended in 1949, Israel held territories beyond the boundaries set by the UN plan. The

UN made no serious attempt to enforce the internationalisation of Jerusalem, which was now divided between Jordan and Israel, and separated by barbed wire fences and no man's land areas. The Arab countries refused to sign a permanent peace treaty with Israel. Consequently, the borders of Israel established by the armistice commission never received *de jure* (legal) international recognition. An uneasy truce emerged that continued until the 1960s. Arab leaders came together to form and support the Palestinian Liberation Organisation, which was encouraged to engage in military action against Israel. Against this background, in mid-May, 1967, the neighbouring Arab states pledged themselves in formal treaties to 'the destruction of Israel'. In anticipation of invasion Israel attacked and won stunning victories over Egypt, Jordan and Syria. On June 11, 1967 a ceasefire was agreed. UN Resolution 242 called for negotiations of a permanent peace between the parties, and for Israeli withdrawal from lands occupied in 1967. In October 1973, Egypt and Syria launched another war against Israel, again resulting in defeat and the conquest by Israel of the Sinai Peninsula. This area was returned to Egypt in 1982 as a result of the Camp David Agreement between Egypt and Israel and a subsequent Peace Treaty in 1979. At the same time as Israel was pursuing peace with Egypt it also initiated a policy of settlement in the 'occupied' territories and Jewish communities were settled in areas of the West Bank and Gaza, and an additional two-hundred thousand Jews were settled in areas of Jerusalem and environs conquered in 1967.

Beginning in 1987, Palestinians in Gaza Strip and the West Bank took their fate into their own hands and engaged in a revolt called the Intifada. This had the effect of securing international media attention to the plight of the Palestinians. The conclusion of the Gulf war in 1991, sustained US political pressure and the ongoing break up of the USSR created a favourable international climate that facilitated negotiations on a resolution of the Palestinian problem. In 1993 and 1995, Israel and the PLO signed the Oslo Declaration of Principle and the Oslo Interim Agreement. A peace treaty was also signed with Jordan in 1994. The peace process with the Palestinians led to the withdrawal of Israeli troops from the Gaza Strip and most cities and towns of the West Bank by early 1996. As the Israelis withdrew, Palestinians took control of these areas. In January 1996, Palestinians in the Gaza Strip and the Palestinian-controlled parts of the West Bank established a government with Yasser Arafat as leader. Negotiations for a final settlement ended in deadlock in July 2000. Palestinians insisted that refugees should have the right to return to Israel, which would produce an Arab majority in Israel. Israel insisted on annexing key portions of the Palestinian areas and on leaving most Jewish settlements intact, and offered only a limited form of Palestinian statehood. Palestinian violence erupted on September 28, 2000 and has continued sporadically since. At the time of writing attempts are being made by US Secretary of State Colin Powell to reinvigorate the peace process and to normalise relations between Israel and the Palestinian Authority.

Ironically, one important point to emerge from our overview of Arab-Jewish relations is that there has not always been conflict between them. For much of their history the two groups have enjoyed reasonably amicable relations. The point that clearly emerges in the twentieth century is that the conflict has been occasioned and sustained by the fact that two groups claim the same physical territory. Conflict over the land has naturally created a legacy of bitterness and animosity that stimulates further conflict. Both sides have legitimate claims and grievances. But what is the role of religion in the conflict? The present division between the protagonists is between Palestinian Muslims and Israeli Jews. Should we not therefore conclude that the conflict is clearly religious? There are problems, however, with rushing to such a conclusion. First, religious Jews in Israel can claim exemption from military service and almost all do, even though military service is compulsory for all other Jews. Religious Jews are not involved directly in the conflict. Secondly, and following on from the first point, most Jews in Israel are 'secular' Jews; they have no religious motivation or little specifically religious loyalty. This reminds us that there is an ambiguity in the notion of Jewish identity. Judaism is both a cultural and a religious identity. Use of a common terminology to describe all Jews disguises the difference between religious and secular Jews. In some ways Palestinian identity is more straightforwardly religious, in that they claim to be Muslim; and clearly much of the support they receive from the Arab world is because they are Muslim. Yet even here appearances can be deceptive. Islam is not a religion in the modern Western sense of the term. Islam is a total philosophy of life with very clear political implications. In fact some Western scholars have accused Islam of being a political ideology masquerading as religion. In other words, for the Palestinian the conflict is religious, but only because the religion of Islam embraces politics in a way that contrasts with modern Western interpretations of religion, where the realm of politics is, for the most part, independent of religion and its influence.

An historical perspective on the conflict also yields inconclusive results. We have the evidence that for many centuries the Jews and the Arabs existed peaceably alongside each other. Yet there is also evidence of a deep division between Jews and Arabs that goes back to Abraham. We are all familiar with the Biblical story of Abraham and Sarah and their desire for a child. The Book of Genesis records how Sarah offered her maidservant, Hagar to Abraham (in the accepted custom) and Ishmael was born; subsequently 'the true heir' Isaac was born to Sarah. Abraham became the 'father' of the Jews and Ishmael who was cast out of the household was 'father' of the Arabs. To complicate matters the present day Palestinians are most likely the Arab descendents of the Philistines, that is, the people that was displaced along with others when the Jews moved into the 'Promised Land' of Israel. There was a clear political and religious conflict at this juncture. This religious element would come to the fore in later centuries when the Arabs converted to Islam and the Jews, although subjugated, were allowed to exist as 'People of the Book' under Muslim rule.

Is the conflict between the Jews and the Palestinians religious or not? It depends on what one means by religion? For the Palestinians it is a religious conflict, but only in an extended sense of religion, that is, in a sense that subsumes politics under religion. But such an interpretation of religion, although once influential in the Western world, is no longer taken seriously, both for theological and for other reasons. The sense in which the conflict for the Jews is religious is more attenuated still. The Jews simply want to secure a homeland where they will find security and peace, a hope that has eluded them as a people for most of their history.

The Northern Ireland conflict

For many commentators on religion the conflict situation in Northern Ireland is an obvious example of a religious conflict. The two sides to the dispute are divided on religious lines: Protestants, who favour the status quo and maintenance of constitutional links with Great Britain, and Roman Catholics, who favour stronger political links with the Republic of Ireland and many of whom would favour the absorption of Northern Ireland into a new united Ireland. At a political level these two groups can also be characterised as Unionists and Nationalists. The 'hardliners' within both groups are referred to as loyalists and republicans respectively. We have already referred to the religious and political situation in Ireland and the division of the country into Northern Ireland and the Republic of Ireland in our discussion of 'Religious Traditions in Ireland' in Chapter 1, and there is little need to go over the same ground again. In addition there are numerous historical studies of 'the Troubles' in Northern Ireland (as the twenty-five years of murder, bombings, intimidation and hostilities are often euphemistically called). As a consequence we will keep our historical overview of the situation to a minimum and concentrate on the issue of the contribution of religion to the conflict.

The establishment of Northern Ireland was opposed by many nationalists. The constitutional issue divided opinion into two predictable camps that aligned along religious lines, Protestants who feared 'Roman' domination in a united Ireland and Catholics who aspired to belong to the Republic of Ireland, where the Catholic Church enjoyed privilege and position reinforced by legislation. Catholics who were opposed to the state of Northern Ireland were naturally unenthusiastic in their support for state institutions and as a result the security forces were almost exclusively Protestant. The Irish Republican Army, the name taken by those who opposed 'British' rule by force, conducted campaigns in the 1920s, 1940s and 1950s, but to little avail and some small loss of life. These campaigns underlined the fact that there were those who wanted to secure a united Ireland by violent means as well as illustrating extreme alienation by some in the Catholic population both from the state in Northern Ireland and the politics of consent. The Protestant majority reacted in predictable ways to what it perceived as disloyalty by Catholics, and inevitably (but wrongly) the violent opposition of some was accredited as guilt to all. Protestants acted to secure their domination and what they believed to be their security. Emergency legislation was introduced on a permanent basis; the police force was impatient of Catholic criticism and openly hostile on occasions to the Catholic community; local government electoral boundaries were openly gerrymandered (a stratagem also used by nationalists when they were able to do so); and economic policies were applied in a way to favour Protestants. Ironically, Catholics did enjoy state support for a confessional school system (as distinct from a secular school system, managed by the state), and this contributed substantially to the emergence of a Catholic middle class in the late 1950s, which in turn prepared the way for civil rights campaigns in the 1960s.

In 1967 the Northern Ireland Civil Rights Association was formed to demand liberal reforms, including the removal of discrimination in the allocation of jobs and houses, permanent emergency legislation and electoral abuses. The campaign was modelled on the civil rights campaign in the United States, involving protests, marches, sit-ins and the use of the media to publicise minority grievances. The local administration was unable to handle the growing civil disorder, and in 1969 the British government sent in troops to enforce order. Initially welcomed by the Catholic population, they soon provided a stimulus for the revival of the republican movement. The newly formed Provisional IRA began a campaign of violence against the army. By 1972 it was clear that the local Northern Irish government, having introduced internment in 1971 as a last attempt to impose control, was unable to handle the situation. Invoking its powers under the Government of Ireland Act, the Westminster parliament suspended the Northern Ireland government and replaced it with direct rule from Westminster. This situation continued into the 1990s.

The IRA campaign developed strongly from 1972: 'no warning' bombs exacted a heavy toll on the civilian population along with a concerted campaign to kill security personnel. Fitfully at first, but with increasing success and commitment, loyalist paramilitary groups responded to republican violence by killing Catholics, along with those believed to be engaged in terrorist activity against the state. Between 1974 and the ceasefires of 1994 there were seven attempts to reach a political and constitutional settlement. All of the initiatives were London-led and included an element of power-sharing between Catholics and Protestants. All foundered in the face of local opposition. There is no need to review subsequent developments and the political path that lead to the signing to the Good Friday/Belfast agreement of April 1998 between the main political parties representative of both traditions. The 'peace process' continues and the cease fires called by the paramilitaries on both sides currently hold.

What part has religion played in the conflict? At one level the conflict is clearly religious. Both sides have waged sectarian violence against the other, where, 'the other' is invariably identified as belonging to a different religion. There are numerous examples in recent times of individuals being murdered for no other reason than the person was perceived as belonging to a different religious tradition. Protagonists to the conflict identity themselves by religious labels and some certainly use the cause of religious loyalty as a means of garnering support from their own respective communities. Moreover, the historical dimension to the Troubles also reveals religion as a prominent factor. Insurrection and massacre, reprisal and 'justice' invariably reveal an element of religious motivation and even an element of formal religious support for violence against those perceived as holding a rival religious position. State enforcement of financial support by Catholics for the Church of Ireland and discriminatory laws against Catholics up until the nineteenth century serve to underline the religious nature of the conflict. Equally, Northern Protestant opposition to a united Ireland in the first few decades of the twentieth century was galvanised by the possibility of a loss of religious freedom in a Catholic state at a time when Catholicism had set its face firmly against liberal democracy and when the state was required by Catholic teaching to enforce Catholic beliefs and Catholic morality.

There are, however, other factors that militate against regarding religion as a dominant factor in the Northern Ireland conflict. It could be argued that two different 'ethnic' groups are engaged in a struggle for economic and political dominance; religion just happens to be one further point of difference between groups engaged in a conflict whose real cause lies elsewhere. One of the biggest challenges to the interpretation of the Northern Ireland conflict as religious is the fact that Catholics and Protestants in other contexts do not engage in violence against each other. Certainly religion may be implicated in the conflict and may have equivocated historically in condemning violence but the real cause is political – British political dominance, Irish assertions of independence, and so on. This suggestion can claim some support from the religious allegiances of those paramilitaries who participate in the conflict and from the general character of society. Few of those who belong to Loyalist paramilitary groups regard themselves as religious. They choose to identify themselves with the Protestant community, but this association is historical and political. Interestingly, when loyalist paramilitaries 'convert' to Christianity, they usually renounce violence and extricate themselves from paramilitary groups. The situation of republican paramilitaries is more ambiguous, in that they typically maintain formal Catholic allegiances and seem to be able to reconcile violence alongside commitment to Christ and his Church. The issues then arise whether the Church is being used as a badge of community identity and whether outward formal commitment correlates to an inner Christian disposition of mind and spirit? At the wider level of society it may be difficult to maintain the thesis that Northern Ireland is a deeply Christian society, a fact, which if true, may give some support to the thesis that the conflict is irreducibly religious. We have already offered some remarks on the secularisation thesis in Ireland in Chapter 1 and questioned the notion that high levels of church attendance in both parts of Ireland necessarily translate into high levels of Christian practice in terms of morality and life style.

Ironically, our consideration of the evidence suggests that a conclusion not unlike that reached with regard to the

Palestinian/Jewish conflict may be equally appropriate. The Northern Ireland conflict is religious in the sense that religion distinguishes the protagonists and that religion concerns are reflected in disputes between the two communities. But equally it is a religious conflict only in an extended sense of religion, that is, in a sense that subsumes politics under religion. If politics has no real substantive connection to religion other than to use religion for ideological purposes, or alternatively if religion is related to politics in a more self-critical way that challenges existing alliances between religion and Northern Irish politics then the conflict may not be religious at all (or perhaps religious in a sense that should be distinguished from the beliefs and practice of authentic Christianity).

8

New Religious Movements

Religions develop and evolve over time. The religion of the Upanishads contrasts with the religion of the Vedas and both are quite different from mainstream Hinduism today. Contemporary Christian belief and practice differs from the Christianity of the Mediaeval period. Continuity is characteristically claimed with the past (for it is this continuity which is regarded by adherents as legitimising contemporary expressions of the religion), but changing circumstances and situations require religions to adapt and transform if they are to maintain relevance and accessibility to a new generation. Religions adapt in different ways in reaction to fresh challenges. In some cases, as in liberal forms of religion, change is welcomed and espoused. In other cases, change occurs grudgingly and reluctantly. The rise of fundamentalist movements within most of the major world religions indicates the extent to which religious identity is historically constituted and constructed: adaptation to the modern world is resisted in the name of 'faithfulness to the received tradition'. But disavowals of change and adaptation, however shrill and sustained, need to be interpreted with caution. The notion of a golden past when religion held free sway over the hearts and minds of people and when religious practice was pure and unadulterated by false motives is easily falsified by the facts of history. Ironically, the idealised picture of a definitive, historical form of religion in the past is, surreptitiously, a mandate for contemporary religious change and development: change and development in a decidedly conservative direction, a calling back of religion to its former 'authentic' glory. Fundamentalism is and remains a uniquely modern manifestation of religion: modernity is resisted in the name of hallowed tradition.

But are there limits to development and adaptation within a religion? Are some forms of religion legitimate and some illegitimate? This is a question that has occupied some of the foremost theological minds over the centuries, though more in the past than the present and more by Western theologians than Eastern thinkers. Right belief or orthodoxy in the West came to be carefully defined in creed and confession, and denial of this right belief amounted to *heresy*: the conscious choice to depart from true faith and doctrine (the term 'heresy' is derived from the Greek word '*hairesis*', literally 'choice'). At some times and in some places denial of the prevailing orthodoxy carried serious consequences. Al-Hallaj, the Sufi mystic and poet of the thirteenth century, after an irregular trial by the religious authorities, was sentenced to death on charges of heresy. Subjected to a terrible scourging, the amputation of his limbs, and exposure on a gibbet, he was finally beheaded, his body burned and his ashes strewn over the Tigris. Christian history has its heretics and its equally barbarous punishments. Thankfully, the advent of the modern world, and the slow but steady wrestling of political power from religious institutions, has diminished the offence of heresy in the eyes of the state, in the West at least. One legacy of the religious wars and conflicts of the sixteenth and seventeenth centuries was the realisation that some form of religious accommodation between professed adherents of the same Christian faith was necessary. Since the sixteenth century, and in part precipitated by the fracture of the Church by the Protestant Reformation, religion has increasingly become a private rather than a public matter. Religious freedom, not unsurprisingly, advanced at greater pace in the Protestant dominated nations of Northern Europe. The right of personal judgement in relation to religious belief, so central to Luther's principled opposition to the Catholicism of his day, naturally but not uncontroversially was slowly extended to allow for the mutual co-existence of different forms of Protestantism within the same territorial boundary. As the centuries advanced so freedom of choice in the matter of religion has become increasingly realised. Some modern, political constitutions still reflect the particular beliefs of one religious tradition, and may even enforce some limited legal adherence to this tradition, but for the most part individuals are free to choose and practise the religion of his or her choice, or even to relinquish religious belief and adherence altogether.

As the state relinquished interest in maintaining religious orthodoxy, so a new climate was created for the development and expression of 'alternative' religious beliefs and spiritualities, that is, alternative beliefs to mainstream Christianity. Of course what counts as mainstream Christianity and alternatives to it are shifting concepts. Different historical periods have construed the application of such terms differently. No doubt, Protestantism was initially a protest movement against mainstream Catholic Christianity, and as it established itself institutionally, politically and socially, so other protest movements arose and distinguished themselves within Protestantism, the different Anabaptists groups for example – Hutterites, Mennonites and the like. This process of religious differentiation within Christianity continues to this day. What is novel about the twentieth century is both the phenomenal increase in the number of alternative religious groups within society in the West and the rise of groups that owe their inspiration and origin to expressly Eastern modes of religious belief and practice. It is this last feature which raises important issues for the student of religion. Prior to the nineteen-sixties, when Eastern forms of spirituality began to win adherents in the West, the conceptual apparatus and terminology used to describe alternative religion and alternative religious movements were drawn from reflection on the process of religious differentiation within Christianity and, moreover, reflected Christian theological concerns. In order to explain the process of differentiation and the emergence of different groups and social identities within Christianity the following concepts were formulated and utilised: Church, cult, sect, and denomination. We will examine each in turn before turning to address the question of their adequacy to describe the recent rise of religious movements and groups in the West whose inspiration and substance are not Christian.

8.1   CHURCH, CULT, DENOMINATION AND SECT

In his famous essay entitled *The Protestant Ethic and the Spirit of Capitalism* Max Weber (1864–1920) introduced a distinction between two different types of religious organisation, that of a Church-type organisation and that of a sect-type organisation. The purpose of it was to help him to explain the nature of social change in Christianity, more specifically, to help him to explain how Protestantism distinguished itself socially from Catholicism and why Protestantism rather than Catholicism provided the intellectual and social context for the emergence of Capitalism. Our focus will fall exclusively on his distinction between a church and a sect. The original Christian Gospel, according to Weber, contained different elements of social organisation in creative tension with each other. The initial impulse of religious enthusiasm expressed in the form of charismatic leadership and intense personal devotion, gave way to a more formal institutionalised structure, which in order to command assent from the wider community, accommodated itself to the prevailing socio-cultural and economic system.

Thus two types of religious organisation emerge. The sect, which sees itself in opposition to the prevailing norms and structures of society, and the Church, which tends to accept the legitimacy of the prevailing social order and works within this order to achieve influence and universal applicability. The attitude of the Church towards the world is marked by accommodation, whereas the sect relates to the world in terms of protest and opposition. According to Weber, both Church and sect types of religious organisation can find support in the life and witness of the early Christian movement.

This Church/sect distinction gives rise to a series of basic oppositions.

- In the Church form of religion there are few or no membership tests and entry qualifications: entry into the people of God is by birth and accordingly infant baptism is common. One is not normally born into a sect, but becomes a member by choice.
- Absolute commitment is demanded of sect members. All of one's life should be ordered by the sect's teaching. Church membership typically makes fewer claims on the commitment of its members. Entirely consistent with this is the observation that sect membership tends to be small whereas Church membership is large and potentially encompasses the whole of society.
- Sects tend to be protest movements and are typically critical of some aspects of Church teaching and practice. Accusations of accommodation with the lax standards of the world, which have been allowed to infiltrate the Church, are frequently voiced.
- The highly structured and bureaucratic nature of Church government is rejected by sects in favour of more informal structures. Sects tend to be lay organisations and even when they do develop a body of religious functionaries and organisers they tend to be anti-sacerdotal. Protestant reform

groups (sects) within the Church almost invariably exalt the principle of 'the priesthood of all believers' over against the perceived hierarchical structure of the Church-type institution.

• Initially sect members tend to come from the lower classes, those who are already predisposed to reject the accommodation with the world and the relatively undemanding life-style espoused by Church-type organisations in their quest for universality.

(The British sociologist, Bryan Wilson, developed a much simpler analysis of sects. He defined sects in terms of the following straightforward features: voluntary, exclusive, provides an elite identity, expulsion is possible, individual conscience is vital, and members must obey the authority structure of the sect.)

Weber's use of the Church/sect typology was chiefly to illuminate the emergence and growth of Capitalism, but others were quick to exploit its potential as a tool for explaining the ongoing history of Christianity as a social movement. Ernst Troeltsch, for example, employed the distinction to interpret the internal history of Christianity from its New Testament beginnings to the late nineteenth century. He argued that during the late mediaeval period, the two organisational types – Church and sect, which had existed in creative tension from the beginning, split apart. The split occurred because the Church form of religious organisation had come to dominate exclusively. The Church had betrayed its spiritual roots in its largely successful attempt to win political power and influence. The split became visible and institutional with the Protestant Reformation: sect against Church. Moreover, within a generation Protestantism began to adopt some of the organisational features of a Church and new Protestant sects were formed in reaction. From the Reformation, the dynamic interplay between Church and sect has assumed different forms and continues to work itself out in the different Christian traditions.

Although there is much to be said for Troeltsch's interpretation of Christian social history, there are those who think that his distinction between a Church and a sect is too sharply drawn. The opposition between a Church and a sect type of religious organisation may have plausibility as a description of how religious movements initially divide to create new groups, but it does not explain how over the course of a few generations the original sect type group tends to moderate both its original opposition towards the Church from which it emerged and its original strident otherworldly character. The basic argument is that sects that emerge from conflict with a Church do not necessarily remain sects for ever, they evolve a more moderate accommodating stance to the original Church and they moderate the demands they place on their followers. In other words, there is a distinctive form of religious organisation that emerges in time from the division between Churches and sects, namely the denomination. On the one hand, denominations are to be distinguished from Church type organisations, and on the other hand, they are to be distinguished from sect type organisations. Ernst Becker described a denomination as 'a sect that has cooled down'. Denominations are characterised by a number of features.

- Unlike a Church, a denomination is smaller and more restricted in its appeal. It tends to attract a middle-class following.
- Unlike a sect, it develops a specialist ministry – a step in the direction of the Church's hierarchical system.
- The denomination differs from both sect and Church in that it acknowledges that other forms of Christianity have their own validity and integrity. Both the sect and the Church think they have a monopoly of religious truth. The Church in its quest for universal acceptance and relevance commends itself

as the only repository of religious truth. The sect in its quest for spiritual vitality and reality opposes the Church's exclusive claim to salvation and endorses an alternative path to salvation. By contrast, denominational forms of Christianity do not claim a monopoly of religious truth.

• Unlike Churches, denominations have no formal connections with the state.

• Typically, denominations are smaller than Churches and larger than sects.

• Denominations take a mediating position between accommodating with the beliefs and values of the world and opposing the beliefs and values of the world. Sects typically oppose mainstream vales and Churches typically support mainstream values.

Alongside use of Weber's Church/sect distinction, Troeltsch also identified a third form of organisation in religion, which he referred to as 'the mystical'. He carefully distinguished mystical forms of religion from sectarian and Church forms, and most present day sociologists of religion have followed him in accepting the validity of this further category, though the category is now more commonly called *cultic* religion. Accordingly, in sociological parlance a cult exhibits the following features:

• It is a loosely knit group organised around some common religious theme, interest or personality, but lacking any sharply defined and exclusive belief system.

• The cult, like the denomination, is tolerant and understanding of its own members. Each individual member of the cult is the final arbiter of what constitutes religious truth and the path to salvation. Individualism and individual decision are is to the fore.

• In keeping with the fact that members choose what to believe for themselves, cultic groups tend to extol personal experience: believe only in that of which one has direct experience.

• Small membership.

Typical cults, on this interpretation, are Transcendental Meditation, the New Age Movement and Spiritualism. I say *on this interpretation* for the term cult is widely used in the media and in common parlance to designate objectionable, authoritarian or potentially exploitative forms of religion. I shall return to this point a little later.

The distinctions between Churches, sects, denominations and cults can now be summarised in a fairly simple model. Much of what we have discussed up to now about the different social forms of Christianity can be illustrated by asking two basic questions: how does the group view its own revelation in relation to other religious groups and how is the group regarded by the wider society. These two questions and the principles which they uncover yield four categories which identify the four main types of Christian social organisation.

	Respectable	Deviant
Uniquely legitimate	CHURCH	SECT
Pluralistically legitimate	DENOMINATION	CULT

Following Roy Wallis, *The Road to Total Freedom: A sociological analysis of Scientology* (London: Heinemann, 1976), p. 13.

The Church and the denomination are equally respectable social institutions, in the sense that the wider society either looks upon them with approval or it does not actively disapprove of them. Membership of both is typically by birth and little by way of active discipleship is required. They differ however in their perception of themselves: the Church regards itself as containing the fullness of religious truth and, in theory at least, believes itself to be uniquely legitimate, it alone provides the means of salvation. By contrast the denomination, for all its distinctiveness of belief and practice, acknowledges that the substance of faith is shared with other religious communities. Both the sect and the cult are regarded as deviant groups by the wider society. The sect consciously opposes the claimed religious monopoly of the Church by an equally uncompromising affirmation of its own religious truth. The social acceptance enjoyed by the Church and its members is viewed by sect members as illustrative of the extent to which the Church has compromised its principles in the effort to secure social acceptance and influence. The sect opposes the Church and the world in the name of Christian discipleship and is opposed in turn. The cult is also viewed by society in deviant terms even though it makes no claim to exclusive truth. Cults tend to exalt personal freedom and experience, and are generally apolitical groups. The wider society often characterises cult beliefs as exotic or bizarre and for this reason cult members are viewed with suspicion and even amusement. This typology of religious organisations leaves aside the issue of religious truth. It is not assumed that Church-type institutions somehow preserve religious truth in a way denied to other types of institutions and organisations. Similarly, to identify some religious group as exemplifying typically sect features does not entail the falsification of its beliefs or values. The typology is in terms of organisational features complemented by the different social perceptions of group members and non-members. It is indifferent to matters of truth or orthodoxy: the terms employed are used in a neutral and descriptive sense.

8.2   SECTS AND CULTS OR NEW RELIGIOUS MOVEMENTS

What light do our distinctions between Churches, sects, denominations and cults throw on religious change and innovation? Do these distinctions illuminate and clarify our increasingly diverse religious terrain or do they confuse? To ask this is immediately to plunge into controversy for scholars and students of religion are divided in their responses. A number of writers maintain that the traditional terminology is still appropriate and illuminative of the social evolution of religion in its increasing diversity. Other writers question whether a distinctive terminology which evolved out of concerns to explain social and religious differentiation *within* Christianity can fruitfully illuminate our current post-Christian religious pluralism. Debate has centred chiefly on the appropriateness of the traditional concepts of sect and cult to contemporary religious groups. Some contend that the proper application of the term 'sect' to describe a particular form of religious social organisation presupposes an established or national Church-type organisation from which the sect has evolved and this in turn presupposes a society where the majority of people are members of this established Church. But these conditions no longer obtain; at least not in the last two to three decades in most countries in Western Europe. Established Churches have evolved into denominations: declining numbers, loss of social significance, and the adoption by society of secular public values have ensured that the once socially dominant type of Church organisation no longer exists. Add to this the fact that many of the new religious groups and communities have not evolved out of Christianity or view themselves as ever having links, however tenuous, with Christianity: examples are the Sufi Order in the West or the International Society for Krishna Consciousness. In what sense should such groups be characterised as sects? Does this designation advance our understanding and interpretation of them?

Use of the term 'cult' has also become controversial among social scientists. The word is widely used in popular discourse to designate unorthodox or unusual religious groups who are believed to pose a threat to the standards and behaviour of mainstream society and who frequently exert undue control over their adherents. To describe a religious group as a cult carries particularly negative connotations among the general public. To take account of this some scholars have suggested that traditional notion of a cult should be reinterpreted to refer to oppressive and totalitarian religious groups. Cults, on this understanding, accentuate the negative features of a sect.

- Total allegiance is required by the cult's powerful (charismatic) leader.
- There is discouragement of rational thought.
- Deceptive recruitment techniques are used.
- Cults tend to manipulate the emotions of members, particularly the emotion of guilt.
- Cults typically isolate their members from non-members.
- Absolute dedication to the movement is required: the dedication of one's work and finances.
- Cults tend to disparage the family unit.

Examples of cults in this sense would be the Branch-Davidian movement in the Unites States, whose headquarters in Waco, Texas, were besieged by police in 1993, the movement that followed Bhagwan Shree Rajneesh, and according to some scholars, the Unification Church. But we are still left with confusion between a descriptive older notion of a cult as a loosely knit, tolerant group and a newer, partly descriptive and partly evaluative, understanding of a cult as an oppressive group.

Reflection on these considerations and mindful of the increasing religious diversity of society convinced some social commentators that it would be better to abandon use of the terms cult and sect altogether (with their associated connotations). During the nineteen-seventies the term New Religious Movements began to be used as a collective category for religious groups and communities who would formerly have been designated as sects or cults. An added advantage was seen in the fact that this new concept could be extended to include those religious groups that did not fit conveniently into the former categories of either sect or cult. Other social commentators have persisted with the traditional terminology or have maintained that the concepts of cult and sect have a meaningful application to developments within Christianity alone. If this counsel is heeded it would mean that the concepts of cult and sect are inappropriate to describe most of the new religious groups or communities which have arisen in society since the nineteen-sixties, given that they are explicitly non-Christian, but are appropriate to explain most of the historical religious developments within Western society prior to this.

There is no simple resolution to this debate on the concepts and terminology best suited to describe religious innovation and change within societies. It might even be that different concepts are appropriate to different societies. In a clearly post-Christian society like Britain the concept of New Religious Movement may well be the best designation to describe non-conventional religious groups. In Ireland, where Christianity still retains social significance, the concepts of sect and cult may still have a meaningful application. It is not necessary to come down firmly on one side of the debate or the other. It is important, however, to be aware of the debate and the considerations which bear upon it. Any terminology that is employed should be carefully defined and explained. If this simple advice were followed, much potential confusion could be avoided. For the remainder of this chapter we shall focus on the concept of New Religious Movements, clarify the type of religious groups which are usefully characterised in this way, and finally look more closely at two representative groups.

A typology of new religious movements

Since 1945 about five hundred 'new' religions have emerged in Britain. Undoubtedly, the number of 'new' religions to win adherents in Ireland over the same period is much smaller, but it nevertheless remains true to say that Ireland is not exempt from the general pattern of increasing religious innovation and diversity. New religious groupings and communities originally came to the fore in Western Europe and North America during the nineteen-sixties in the counter-culture movement, with its emphasis upon freedom, spontaneity and self-expression. Many young people, dissatisfied with the materialism and wasteful consumerism of Western society and equally dissatisfied with orthodox Christian responses to global and moral issues, which were predictably conservative, sought religious experience elsewhere. Some sought a spirituality that embraced environmental concerns, while others turned to Eastern thought (following the example of the Beatles) in the quest for authenticity in religion. There was even an interest in the ancient pre-Christian religions of Europe, Wicca and Druidism, for example. This interest in novel forms of religious expression has increased over the years. A recent commentator on the religious situation in Britain noted that it offers 'a supermarket of faiths' from which to choose.

The sheer range and diversity of the new religious groups present in modern Britain and Ireland makes it difficult to characterise them as a whole. Is there any way to structure and interpret New Religious Movements that will bring some order to this diversity? According to the British scholar Roy Wallis, New Religious Movements can be divided into three broad categories or ideal-types, namely, world-affirming, world-rejecting and world-accommodating. World-affirming movements are essentially individualistic, locating the source of the suffering that they seek to overcome within oneself, not in society. They have a particularly clear focus on the self and its experience. Individual experience has priority over group experience, and the group serves to advance the experience of the individual. Accordingly, such groups lack collective rituals or conventional religious structures and adherents may not have a particularly strong sense of group attachment. World-affirming movements include Transcendental Meditation (TM), Scientology, and many of the psycho-therapeutically based groups often bracketed together under the heading of 'Human Potential Movements'. Wallis' world-rejecting category includes most of the more recognisably religious groups such as International Society of Krishna Consciousness, the Unification Church and the Children of God. These are groups that segregate themselves from mainstream society and its 'corrupt' values. Finally, the world-accommodating category includes groups allegedly content with or indifferent to the present world order, focusing instead on gaining either solace or fulfilment in the interior, personal life. In this group Wallis includes groups such as Subud, a Muslim mystic movement introduced to the West by an Indonesian, Pak Subuh, the Charismatic renewal movement within Christianity, as well as some more esoteric groups.

Although Wallis' typology has been widely influential it is not without its critics. The various New Religious Movements, it is objected, do not in fact fit into such clear-cut categories, often being internally inconsistent and thus appearing 'world-affirming', 'accommodating' or 'rejecting' at different points or when viewed from different perspectives. One might retort that Wallis' typology highlights one significant aspect of new religious groups, that of the relationship of the group to the wider social reality. Are not all generalisations subject to some qualification? An alternative way of characterising New Religious Movements has been pursued by another British scholar, Michael Parsons. He proposes that new religions should be grouped loosely around similar sorts of origin or interest. He proposes three such broad and inclusive groups of New Religious Movements. First, there are New Religious Movements that are clearly and straightforwardly derived from traditional world religions. Such groups should properly be regarded as varieties of Hinduism, Islam, Christianity, and so on. As examples, Parsons quotes the International Society for

Krishna Consciousness (derived from Hinduism), the Friends of the Western Buddhist Order, and the Jesus Army (Christianity). A second group of New Religious Movements, although identifiably related to the major religious traditions, are in his opinion manifestly so different and distinctive that they are no longer plausibly classifiable as part of the 'parent' tradition. In this category Parsons includes the Children of God, a communal, highly authoritarian, superficially Christian movement under the leadership of David ('Mo') Berg; the Unification Church, which claims to complete Christianity by the teachings of its founder, former Korean Presbyterian, Reverend Sun Myung Moon; the Divine Light Mission associated with Guru Maharaj Ji; and the Transcendental Meditation movement associated with Maharishi Mahesh Yogi. The third and largest group of New Religious Movements proposed by Parsons is, he acknowledges, harder to define and even broader in its scope than the two other groups. This group is broadly clustered around the richly varied collection of 'self-religions', psychotherapies, New Age mysticisms and alternative spiritualities. It may, he suggests, be broadly divided into two sub-groups, each of which is simply a clustering of often quite diverse movements around a similar overall theme. The first sub-group consists of the 'self-religions' and religiously 'flavoured' psycho-therapies which have increasingly flourished in the last few decades. It includes, for example, certain kinds of encounter group, more formal organisations such as Exegesis and Scientology, and groups such as rebirthing or *est* which emphasise positive thinking. The second sub-group consists of 'New Age religions', which combine a quest for inner peace and harmony with more tangible concerns for transcendent realities or to the environment as a whole. As examples of New Age phenomena Parsons cites alternative medicines and healing techniques which are linked to concepts of reincarnation or spiritual evolution; alternative spiritualities and beliefs which draw upon ancient pagan, psychic, astrological or occult traditions.

It is not necessary to adjudicate between the relative merits of Parsons' and Wallis' typologies. Both have their strengths and weaknesses. Wallis' typology distinguishes groups on the basis of their attitude towards the wider society and its values. By contrast, Parsons' typology distinguishes New Religious groups on the basis of their peculiarly religious features: the way in which New Religious Movements expedite religious experience, broadly interpreted, and the way in which they consciously borrow or are historically derived from the major world religions. Both typologies can be regarded as complementary to each other for both help us to understand and conceptualise the increasingly diverse nature of religion in contemporary society.

We will conclude this chapter by looking at two New Religious Movements, the New Age Movement and the International Society of Krishna Consciousness.

The New Age Movement
The New Age Movement is an umbrella term for a wide diversity of beliefs and practices, broadly of a spiritual nature, which has come to the fore in recent years, and which while being religious in character, does not conform to traditional Christian teaching. The movement can be described as 'an alternative spiritual tradition', that is, an alternative to the more familiar, and until recently in the West, the culturally dominant, Judaeo-Christian tradition. The term 'New Age' expresses the movement's hope and explicit purpose of inaugurating a new era in human history that will be marked by universal brotherhood and a new harmony between humankind and nature.

This desire for a new era to emerge for humankind is typically optimistic, and part of this optimism relates to the claim made by some astrologers that we should be entering the

Age of Aquarius. According to astrology, the earth is on a 26,000 year cycle, and approximately every 2,100 years there is a purely astrological shifting of the vernal equinox through a new constellation of the zodiac: each particular star constellation exerts a different influence over human affairs. Therefore, human history reveals a pattern conforming to the influence of the different star constellations. On this scheme of things, the Age of Pisces, for which Christianity was the appropriate religious expression (the fish being an early symbol of Christianity because its letters in Greek were taken as an acronym for a number of prominent New Testament titles of Jesus), should now be giving way to the Age of Aquarius, 'the water bearer'. In the popular musical of the sixties, 'Hair', we find the words: 'when the moon is in the seventh house, and Jupiter aligns with Mars, then peace will guide the planets, and love will fill your hearts'. The Age of Aquarius is to be characterised by love, universal brotherhood and the full realisation of humankind's natural spiritual powers. The hope of the New Age movement for a new era in human consciousness and history to emerge claims support from astrology; and astrology in turn provides a doorway into New Age ideas and practices.

The immediate origins of the New Age movement are to be found in the hippie sub-culture or counter culture of the nineteen-sixties, with its rejection of traditional patterns of behaviour and authority, and of course *traditional* religion, with its commitment to conservative political values and an austere personal ethic. Yet the rejection of religion was not complete, for within the hippie movement, as is well known, there was a widespread desire for religious or transcendent experience: religious experience divorced from orthodox religion, which many were encouraged to believe could be gained by psychedelic or mind altering drugs, and religious experience which consciously looked to Eastern forms of religious expression and spirituality for inspiration. While the hippie movement, and the broader counter-culture of which it was an important part, has not survived in anything like its original form, some of its distinctive emphases and values have been incorporated into mainstream culture and society. The widespread interest in peace groups and organizations, opposition to nuclear power and preoccupation with conservation and green issues are all concerns which came to the fore in the late sixties and were originally part of the counter-culture's critique of a materialistic and consumer-orientated society. There are other factors at work which have prepared the way for a new radical alignment between society and religion, that is, religion in the form of the New Age movement. One could mention the increasing disenchantment with the established political order, the desire for community, and the hope that new patterns of work and leisure will emerge which can overcome the sense of alienation which is a characteristic feature of much modern urban life.

The New Age movement has no single founder and no official creed or articles of belief, rather it draws inspiration from a number of different historical and contemporary writers and individuals. Prominent spokespersons for the New Age movement are the actress Shirley MacLaine, the physicist Fritjof Capra, Sir George Trevelyan, founder of the Wrekin Trust, and the North American theologian, Matthew Fox. The movement also looks for inspiration to earlier thinkers and writers whose ideas have now, as it were, come of age. In this connection one can mention Helena Blavatsky (1831–91) and Alice Bailey (1880–1949): to an earlier generation the writings of both would have been referred to as theosophical. Some recent commentators have suggested that the New Age movement is best thought of as a network: a web or network of interconnected groups, organisations and individuals, bound together by overlapping goals and objectives. One other way to characterise the New Age movement is to focus on the spiritual practices and activities associated with it. Again there is the problem of selection, for most of the practices are not new or unique to the New Age position. New Age thinkers draw on the long contemplative tradition of spiritual exercises and training, propounded and practised by adherents of the different religions, and particularly prominent in the Eastern religions of Hinduism and Buddhism. Practices and activities that seem to be characteristic of the movement are: astral projection, automatic writing, astrology and the use of horoscopes, channelling and the claim to have Spirit guides, colour therapy, divination, perhaps in the form of consulting the *I Ching* or Tarot cards, dream analysis, mind-altering techniques such as chanting and yoga, some of the practices connected with alternative medicine, say the use of crystals and acupuncture. A small number within the movement would advocate more openly pagan (for the most part reviving pre-Christian religious practices) and occult practices, such as the practice of black magic.

Although there is great diversity within the New Age movement there are common emphases: a dissatisfaction with the materialism and secularism of much modern advanced industrialised society; an equal dissatisfaction with conventional religion; a holistic approach to life and health; a shared vision of a new world order; and the conviction that each of us has a natural human and spiritual capacity to effect change in ourselves and in the wider world. But can one go further than this and identify a characteristically New Age worldview? A certain amount of caution is needed here. It would indeed be difficult to find a label that encompassed all the practices associated with the New Age Movement. Yet ironically, the diversity that characterises New Age though is strikingly similar to the diversity that characterises Hinduism. In Hinduism we find a myriad of spiritual beliefs, practices and ideas, from astrology to consulting a spirit-guide, to contemplating the divine essence that is present in all things. It is this notion of a supreme Spirit, Brahman, latent in all things that gives a unifying centre to Hinduism, and it is such a concept of the divine that similarly provides a unifying centre for the New Age Movement. When everything is thought to subsist in the divine, then anything can become a focus for the divine; though of course some activities and objects are more transparent to the divine or more relevant to particular individuals than others. On this understanding, religious practices and activities can be graded according to the extent to which the inherent divinity of all things is recognised. The more rudimentary and simple one's religious awareness is, the more the divine is confined to particular objects and locations and the more advanced one's religious awareness is, the more inclusive one becomes in identifying objects, practices and locations with the divine. In this way simple, and even superstitious, religious practices can be accorded a positive religious function; as steps on the way to a deeper understanding.

According to a number of American commentators interest and support for the New Age is in marked decline. Interestingly one of the chief reasons for this is that the anticipated 'new age' which was to dawn some time in the last few decades has not happened. Anticipation of the arrival of a new spiritual age, where a sense of community and fraternity would overwhelm humankind and lead to new participative structures of world government, has evaporated under the crush of reality. Of course there are other aspects of New Age thought, the variety of spiritual practices, for example, and these continue, albeit with fewer 'clients'. Again there is evidence that the number of those engaging in New Age practices is declining, as the popular market moves on to explore other avenues to self-fulfilment. There will still be those who engage in such activities as channelling, meditation and yoga in the quest for spiritual transformation. But overall, the original hope of the New Age Movement has not been fulfilled: the Age of Aquarius, with its promise of universal brotherhood and the full realisation of humankind's spiritual powers, has failed to arrive.

International Society for Krishna Consciousness

The International Society for Krishna Consciousness (ISKCON) or the Hare Krishna movement is probably one of the most readily recognisable and well known 'alternative' religions in Western Europe and America. Many are familiar with its members attempting to distribute literature on the streets. Full members of ISKCON are distinguished by their dress: men wear dhotis and women wear saris. Members become part of a new family and they often live in the ISKCON temple or a community house in the most basic monastic conditions. Single persons are segregated by sex; married persons live in separate accommodation. Married couples are to have sex only for procreation. Members or initiates are required to give up drugs, illicit sex, and material possessions (in recent years this last requirement has been relaxed somewhat). Their lives are dedicated to the worship of Lord Krishna and attracting others to his service. Lord Krishna is a traditional Hindu deity and although ISKCON is a New Religious Movement in the West its roots are firmly rooted in the bhakti (devotional) traditions of the Indian sub-continent.

The movement's origins can be traced to the arrival in the United States in 1965 of A. C. Bhaktivedanta Swami Prabhupada (1896–1977), a Hindu spiritual master and teacher, who was devoted to Lord Krishna, following the traditions of the Vaisnavas of Bengal, especially the example of Caitanya (1496–1583). According to Caitanya, devotion to Krishna takes precedence over most other religious duties set forth in the Vedas. In the years prior to Prabhupada's departure for America, he had raised a family and involved himself in religious activities. In 1944 he started publishing *Back to Godhead,* a magazine, which he would later use to promote his movement in America. At the age of fifty-nine he became a *sannyasin* (wandering holy man) and retired from family life to concentrate on spiritual matters. In obedience to the last wishes of his revered teacher, Saraswati, he travelled to the United States to enjoin the worship of Lord Krishna.

On arrival in New York, Prabhupada soon began to attract adherents with his dancing and chanting of Hare Krishna, particular those who were disillusioned with the consumerism and competitiveness of American society. Within a short time, he and a number of followers (devotees) established a small temple on Second Avenue; there he led studies on the Bhagavad Gita. During his first year Prabhupada initiated nineteen disciples into the International Society for Krishna Consciousness, the name he gave to his new religious community. After a short time he moved to San Francisco, and established a temple in the Haight Ashbury district, which was then emerging as the centre of the hippie movement. In the next two years ISKCON recruited an estimated 150 to 200 new converts. A communal structure evolved in order to provide food and accommodation for new recruits who had only recently migrated to the area, and who were without permanent or stable residences. This initiative served as a model for the many disciples who were sent to other cities across America to establish Krishna temples and recruit members. Being a missionary movement, ISKCON was opportunistic in its recruitment strategies, successfully recruiting in public places and appealing particularly to the disillusioned middle-classes. By the end of 1975, ISKCON had established nearly forty communities and preaching centres in North America and many more worldwide. Economically, ISKCON was largely supported by *sankirtana,* the public distribution of religious literature. Within a decade, Prabhupada and his followers had established a worldwide movement. He focused his energies on translating and writing commentaries on ancient Vedic scriptures such as the Bhagavad Gita and the Srimad Bhagavatam, which were published by Bhaktivedanta Book Trust, the publishing house he established in Los Angeles. Before his death in 1977, Prabhupada had initiated nearly five thousand disciples into Krishna consciousness and attracted tens of thousands of other less-committed followers.

The key belief of the International Society for Krishna Consciousness is that Krishna is the supreme Lord of the universe. Recitation of the names of Krishna, i.e., the Krishna chant or mantra, brings one into union with God and releases his power in your life.

> Hare Krishna, Hare Krishna, Krishna, Krishna, Hare, Hare,
> Hare Rama, Hare Rama, Rama, Rama, Hare, Hare.

Another core belief of Hare Krishnas is reincarnation, a familiar Indian doctrine. Death is viewed as a transition, not an end. How one behaves in this life will determine one's future rebirth. The goal is to break free from the endless cycle of rebirths, called samsara. This can be achieved only by devotion to God, leading to Krishna Consciousness or union with Krishna, hence 'back to Godhead'. Hell is a temporary destination for people who have sinned greatly on earth.

There are 'Nine Acts of Devotional Service,' that should be performed each day.

- Hearing about God.
- Chanting God's names.
- Remembering God by associating with devotees and reading.
- Serving the Lord Krishna in the temple.
- Worshipping God by bringing others to see his image and preparing food as an offering for Lord Krishna.
- Praying to God.
- Encouraging other people to chant God's names.
- Developing a personal, intimate relationship with God.
- Offering our talents and bodies to God's service.

Hare Krishnas condemn meat-eating, intoxication, illicit sex, and gambling. Since ISKCON is so strongly opposed to meat eating, they practise a strict vegetarian lifestyle. Great importance is attached to the preparation of food, which is offered to God and then eaten as an act of communion. Ritual eating is believed to purify the body of the devotee and prepare him or her for union with Krishna.

The late 1970s and the 1980s was a period of decline and change within ISKCON. Recruitment declined significantly and ISKCON witnessed a sharp downturn in its economic fortunes. Prabhupada's death, in 1977, only intensified ISKCON's decline as the movement faced years of conflict and instability in North America. Following his death there were defections and schism. Controversy broke out over the issue of leadership and succession. There were allegations of drug use and weapons violations in the Berkeley Temple, which resulted in the expulsion of Guru Hansaduta, a prominent leader in the movement. During 1986 and 1987, three other gurus were forced to resign their guruships after charges of sexual misconduct were brought against them. Book distribution declined to well below a half of what it had been at the time of Prabhupada's death. The corresponding decline in revenues had a serious effect on ISKCON communities. In an effort to ward off bankruptcy and to bring much-needed revenue into its communities, ISKCON developed a number of alternative economic strategies. In addition to distributing books in public places, devotees began to sell record albums, artwork, candles, and food.

With declining finances, ISKCON found it difficult to sustain its segregated, communal life-style. Many members had little choice but to seek ordinary (secular) employment. Segregation gave way to more flexible and inclusive boundaries as the movement sought to align itself with conventional culture and society. The need to undertake work in the 'outside' world meant that there was less time for religious devotions. The duties of employment, family responsibilities, educating children, and the like, now largely define the daily concerns of the average ISKCON member and not devotions. Everyday reality has forced ISKCON members to recraft their identities to reflect their involvement in two social worlds previously regarded as hostile to one another. ISKCON's social structure has had to change accordingly and there has been a shift from a narrowly based monastic organisation to that of a broad based, pluralistic community.

ISKCON has around a dozen centres throughout the United Kingdom and the Republic of Ireland. Apart from a small community of about half-a-dozen families who meet in each other's homes in Wicklow there are three main ISKCON communities at present in Ireland – one in Dublin, one in Belfast, Dunmurray, and one on Inis Rath (Hare Krishna Island) in Upper Lough Erne, County Fermanagh.

The ISKON community in Northern Ireland is small and has grown slowly, though steadily, over the years. There are about twenty-five members living in the two temples and around one hundred congregational members in all. Worship at the temples is conducted on a daily basis by residents and by devotees who live nearby. Inis Rath or Hare Krishna Island serves as a retreat centre for groups and individuals throughout Ireland. Residential courses are available and visitors are welcome. The Temple Room on Inis Rath has recently been renovated in traditional Vedic style with arches and rich decoration. Pictures of Krishna adorn the walls and a large silver and gold-plated altar, with images of Krishna, dominates the room.

Membership at the new Temple (opened in 1986) in Dunmurray is drawn from both Roman Catholic and Protestant backgrounds. Nearly all had stopped practising the religion of their birth before encountering ISKCON, but there are some who have added Krishna Consciousness to their original religious tradition, a practice which is by no means unique according to research carried out in the United States. The Hare Krishna Cultural Centre in Dublin was first opened in the mid-nineteen-seventies, and became firmly established at its present premises in the city centre in 1982. The Centre comprises a shop for the sale of artefacts and items of clothing, a Temple Room, and accommodation and facilities for the full-time members in residence. Whatever their social or national origin, members are given a new Sanskrit name upon membership. The centre-piece of the Temple Room is the main shrine displaying prints of Lord Krishna and other deities. The musical instruments for use in worship – drum, bells, sitar are displayed beside the shrine. Around the walls are scriptural texts and prints depicting different incarnations of Krishna. In one corner stands a symbolic 'throne' used solely to hold a framed portrait of His Divine Grace A. C. Bhaktivedanta Swami Prabhupada, who brought the tradition to the West. To one side of the throne are copies of the Bhagavad Gita on shelves, while above hangs a banner displaying the famous Hare Krishna mantra in silver lettered plates. Seating is in the form of low stools and mats scattered around the tiled floor. Worship in the form of devotion to Krishna is a regular and daily activity at the Dublin temple. The day begins at 4.30am with worship of the deity; from 5am to 5.30am readings and prayers are said; the next two hours are spent in individual chanting using (prayer) beads; this is followed by further collective worship and study of a sacred Hindu text alongside a commentary by Prabhupada. Devotions should be finished by nine o'clock. Part of the day is often spent in witnessing to Krishna on the streets: chanting, distributing literature and engaging in discussions with members of the public. Public meetings are arranged for the evenings or members may socialise or worship together.

9

Other Living Religions

In this chapter we will consider the main beliefs and values of a number of religious groups: the Baha'i faith, Chinese Religion, the Sikh religion and African Traditional Religion. No attempt will be made to be comprehensive.

The Baha'i faith

The Baha'i faith is the youngest of the world's independent religions. Its founder, Baha'u'llah (1817–1892), is regarded by Baha'is as the most recent in a line that stretches back and includes Abraham, Moses, Buddha, Zoroaster, Christ and Muhammad. The central theme of Baha'u'llah's message is that humanity is one single family and that the day has come for its unification in one global society. God, Baha'u'llah said, has set in motion historical forces that are breaking down traditional barriers of race, class, creed, and nation that will, in time, give birth to a universal civilisation. The principal challenge facing the peoples of the earth is to accept the fact of their oneness and to assist the process of unification.

Adherents and distribution

The Baha'i faith is ranked as one of the world's ten largest international religious bodies. Its headquarters are in Haifa,

Israel. Most recent published estimates of the world Baha'i population attribute about six and a half million adherents. The majority of Baha'is live in India, about one and three quarter million, though given the size of India's population, they account only for 0.17 per cent of the total population. Three quarters of a million live in the United States. As a percentage of the total population, Bolivia has the highest concentration of Baha'is – 3.25 per cent and 269,246 adherents. In Africa there are concentrations of Baha'is in Chad and Zambia. As with most religious groups, organisationally reported adherent counts include significant numbers of nominal members, or people who no longer actively participate, yet still identify themselves as adherents. In the case of the Baha'i faith the proportion of nominal members is probably considerably fewer than in some other religions; this is because many Baha'is are converts: it was not the religion of their parents or the majority religion of the surrounding culture. The Baha'i community is remarkably active and influential in religious matters on both global and local levels, especially given their relatively small numbers compared with some other religions.

The origins of the tradition
In 1844, Sayyid Ali Muhammad, a Persian Muslim, proclaimed himself to have special access to the Twelfth or Hidden Imam of Shi'a Islam. For this reason he called himself the *Bab*, the 'door' or 'gate.' Although his message was welcomed enthusiastically by many, he was opposed by the official teachers of Islam. As a result he was arrested and imprisoned for heresy, and finally executed in 1850. Before the Bab died he foretold the coming of someone much greater than he, who would bring deliverance and fulfil God's purpose for the world. His proclamation founded a new religion, Babism. In 1852, two followers of the Bab attempted to assassinate the Shah of Persia. As a conseqence, the leader of the movement, Baha'u'llah, which is Arabic for 'Glory of God' (real name

Mízra Husayn-Ali) was imprisoned, even though he was unconnected with the crime. While in prison, Baha'u'llah received a revelation from God proclaiming that he was the Promised One of God. On release from prison he was exiled to Baghdad. Some years later in 1863, immediately before his departure from Baghdad for Istanbul, he publicly announced his status as God's Special Servant. During his lifetime he was repeatedly exiled from one city to another. He was exiled from Istanbul to Edirne (now Adrianople), where he proclaimed to the world through a series of letters to world leaders that he was the Promised One foretold by the Bab. In 1868, the Turkish authorities exiled Baha'u'llah to Akka, a port city in Syria. He and his followers faced increasing persecution for their unorthodox beliefs. Despite opposition the movement grew. After his death in 1892, Baha'u'llah was succeeded by his son, Abbas Effendi. Known by his followers as Abdu'l-Baha, he oversaw the teaching and spread of the Baha'i faith. His grandson, Shoghi Effendi became the 'Guardian' of the Baha'i community upon his grandfather's death.

The teachings of the tradition
The Baha'i faith believes there is only one God who is transcendent and ineffable. He has been revealed throughout history by a number of divine messengers, who are all manifestations of the divine spirit. The latest of these divine messengers was Baha'u'llah whose role, along with past messengers, was to educate humanity. Since all religions and religious texts come from God, Baha'is study these texts to see how Baha'u'llah fulfils earlier prophecies. The year in which the Bab received his message from God, 1844, is pivotal. For the Baha'is this year coincides with humanity coming to spiritual maturity. Baha'is believe that the old world order is in the process of crumbling and giving way to a world in which the principles of Baha'i will be universally accepted.

Some basic Baha'i faith principles are:

- Each must discover the truth for himself or herself.
- The essential oneness of the human race.
- The essential unity of the different religions.
- The harmony of science and religion.
- The equality of the sexes.
- The positive contribution of education to resolving conflicts and overcoming social injustice and the different forms of prejudice.
- Humankind should work for the abolition of both extreme wealth and poverty.
- Universal peace is achievable through co-operation between nations.

The lifestyle of believers today
There are no set worship services and no ordained priesthood, so members learn about their faith through reading and weekly gatherings. Devotional programmes are simple and typically include prayers, meditations, and readings from the sacred scriptures of their religion and of other world religions. The Baha'i Scriptures consist of the writings of the three central figures at the origin of the tradition: the Bab, Baha'u'llah, and Abdu'l-Baha. Each Baha'i must study the Scriptures and interpret them for himself. Baha'is are also encouraged to appropriate the spiritual riches of other religions and confirm the viewpoint that the same God has been active in revealing himself through all religions. Most Baha'i gatherings take place in people's homes. Small regular meetings in homes for discussion are known as Firesides; those outside the tradition are welcome to attend. Work is an integral part of their faith and is considered part of their daily worship. Having a job is seen as serving the community. Since there is no hierarchy in the Baha'i faith, Baha'u'llah created the Adminstrative Order, a set of guidelines for the running of Baha'i councils at local,

national and world levels. To form a Local Spiritual Assembly a community must have a minimum of nine members over twenty-one years of age. Local Spiritual Assemblies are given responsibility for making decisions on all matters of common action on the part of the community. Each year nine people are elected to serve the community. All Baha'is over twenty-one have the right to vote and to serve on the Assembly if elected. Baha'is follow the laws of the Ten Commandments. They also forbid gambling, alcohol, drug abuse, and gossip. They strive to live a life of high moral standards emphasising honesty, trustworthiness, service to others, and chastity before marriage. Community celebrations include an annual fasting time and eight other holy days in remembrance of events in the lives of the founders. New Year's Day is celebrated on March 21. On holy days, Baha'is do not work and this is considered a sacrifice.

Conflict and Persecution
Since the beginning of the Baha'i faith it has faced resistance and persecution within Iran. Many Baha'is have become martyrs and many are imprisoned due to the current Iranian government's intolerance. Iranian Muslim leaders feel threatened by the Baha'i faith and have acted upon their fears. The Shi'ite clergy views the Baha'is as heretics. Some Baha'i beliefs conflict with Islamic doctrines. Baha'is affirm that there were more prophets after Muhammad; that the Qur'an has been abrogated in favour of Baha'u'llah's writings; that women should play an active role in society; that no importance should be attached to the concept of holy war (*jihad*); and that imams or teachers are not essential to authentic religion. Anti-Baha'i sentiment increased under Ayatollah Khomeini and decreased slightly after his death in the late nineteen-eighties. Baha'is are often accused of prostitution because their marriages are viewed as illegitimate by the state and of being Zionist supporters because their headquarters are in Haifa, Israel.

Baha'is deny the authority of Shi'ite jurisprudence and therefore the essence of Iran's government.

Baha'is in dialogue
According to Baha'is the basis for religious dialogue is the conviction that the same God is revealed in and through the religious texts of humankind. They believe in God and in an after-life and for this reason they view the monotheistic religions as natural dialogue partners. Their small numbers in the West, however, have meant that there has been little official dialogue or conversations between Baha'is and others. At a local level they are keen to enter into dialogue and to work on joint social and humanitarian projects with the churches. Quite often their overtures are rejected. In Muslim countries Baha'is are often persecuted because they are viewed as a heretical sect within Islam that should be suppressed.

Chinese Religion
There are five major religions/philosophies in China: Taoism, Confucianism, Buddhism, Islam and Christianity. Among them, Taoism and Confucianism are uniquely Chinese; for this reason we will confine our attention to them. Both arose at about the same time in the fifth century BCE. Neither was originally a religion in the traditional sense. Confucianism originally reiterated traditional Chinese, moral values and Taoism sought to harmonise humankind with the natural order. These two philosophies, however, developed into popular religions eventually. A word of qualification, however, is necessary at the outset. Although Taoism and Confucianism can be distinguished in terms of their historical origins and fundamental beliefs, in contemporary practice the boundary between the two is blurred.

Adherents and distribution
It is very difficult to give accurate numbers of the adherents of Confucianism and Taoism. The figure for Confucianism is usually cited as between five to six million, with a

concentration in China and the Far East – Korea and Japan, for example. The numbers subsumed under Chinese Traditional religion, however, is typically over two hundred million and we can presume that most of these will combine Confucian ideas with other philosophical and religious ideas. At the level of folk or popular religion religious ideas are conflated and combined: there are no religious boundaries that distinguish one set of beliefs and practices from another.

Taoism is usually cited as having about thirty million adherents, again concentrated in the Far East, particularly Taiwan. It is more clearly religious and more easily distinguished than Confucianism.

The origins, development and teaching of Taoism

Tao (pronounced 'dow') can be roughly translated into English as 'path', or 'the way'. It refers to a power that envelops, surrounds and flows through all things, living and non-living. The Tao regulates natural processes and nourishes balance in the Universe. It embodies the harmony of opposites (i.e. there would be no love without hate, no light without dark, no male without female). The founder of Taoism is believed by many to be Lao-Tse (604–531 BCE), a contemporary of Confucius. He was searching for a philosophy that would avoid the constant feudal warfare that disrupted society during his lifetime. The result was his book, the Tao-te-Ching, 'The Way of Power,' or 'The Book of the Way, from which of course the tradition gets its name. The Tao Te Ching describes the nature of life, the way to peace, and how a ruler should lead his life. The book itself is very short. It is only five thousand characters long, contained in eighty-one chapters. It is divided into two parts: the Tao-ching and the Te-ching. At an early stage it is possible that these two texts existed separately, however, at some time they were translated together and became one book. Chuang-tzu (named after its author) is the second most important Taoist text. The Chuang-tzu contains additional teachings relevant to Taoism. It describes Taoist philosophy in greater detail and contains stories of Taoist masters and disciples. The Chuang-tzu highlights techniques that focus on breathing, meditation, sexual activity, and diet. The date of its composition is uncertain, estimates usually place it sometime in the fourth century BCE. Taoism started as a combination of psychology, philosophy and reflection on the nature of wisdom, and gradually evolved into a religious faith. In 440 CE it was adopted as the state religion of China and Lao-Tse became popularly venerated as a deity.

The Tao is the path that one should follow in life. The Tao is the natural order of things and is based on the principles of Yin and Yang. Taoists believe that the Tao is the universal life force or the underlying nature of all things that exist in the world. Although Taoism is sometimes classified as a polytheistic religion, this description should be interpreted carefully. This is because each of the gods is believed to be a manifestation of some aspect of the Tao. Taoists, however, rarely pray to any of the gods. There is no god that can solve the problems of life. Rather, Taoists seek the solutions to life's problems through personal meditation and mindfulness. According to the Tao Te Ching the basic problem that we all face is that we do not know who we truly are. According to Taoism human beings are caught up in a cosmic process of being and becoming. In life our fundamental choice is either to acknowledge the reality of the Tao that flows through all things or to resist what we are and attempt to establish our own separate identities outside of the Tao. Taoists believe that the world we experience is the manifestation of the eternal Tao. The pattern of the Tao is one of return. In other words, it is a process of coming into being, maturing, and then decaying and returning to the Tao. Everything in the world is a part of this constant cycle. All things possess their own *te* or 'destiny'. When this *te* is not opposed it will naturally manifest itself in the process of life.

The idea of non-action or *Wu Wei*, understood as allowing things to follow their natural process, is a fundamental belief of Taoism; it is not, however, to be equated with passive activity, it is rather action that conforms to the rhythm of the universe: action that conforms to the eternal Tao and is in harmony with nature. Yin and Yang are considered to be complementary aspects of the Tao. Yin is a feminine energy. It is regarded as the breath that formed the earth. It is represented by cold, evil, dark, and negative forces. Yang is masculine energy. It is regarded as the breath that formed the heavens. It is characterised by warmth, goodness, light, and positive forces. It is important to note that without Yin there is no Yang and without Yang there is no Yin. Everything in nature must have both Yin and Yang. These two are not polar opposites but complementary aspects of the Tao. In following the principle of Wu Wei one accomplishes one's goals without effort. A person who lives by Wu Wei has rediscovered his or her original nature. This state is likened to that of an uncarved block and is referred to as *Pu*. Lao Tzu believed that following the principle of Wu Wei would lead to a peaceful and harmonious society.

The origins, development and teaching of Confucianism
Confucius, whose Chinese name was Kong Qiu, lived from 551 to 479 BCE. Confucius sought a revival of the ideas and institutions of a past golden age. Employed in a minor government position as a specialist in the civic and family rituals of his native state, Confucius hoped to disseminate knowledge of the rites and rituals, and to inspire their performance. The transformation of society, he believed, could take place only with the active encouragement of responsible rulers. The ideal ruler, as exemplified by the legendary sage-kings Yao and Shun, had the ability to influence others by the power of moral example. Each individual, in emulation of the ruler, is supposed to cultivate a range of virtues: benevolence toward others, a general sense of doing what is right, loyalty

and diligence in serving one's superiors. Universal moral ideals are necessary but not sufficient conditions for the restoration of civilization. Society also needs what Confucius calls *li*, roughly translated as 'ritual'. People need to develop the ability to act appropriately in any given social situation and to perform the correct rituals, which in turn vary considerably, depending on age, social status, gender, and context. In family rituals, for example, rites of mourning depend on one's kinship relation to the deceased. In international affairs, degrees of pomp, as measured by ornateness of dress and opulence of gifts, depend on the rank of the foreign emissary. Offerings to the gods are also highly regulated: the sacrifices of each social class are restricted to particular types of deities, and a clear hierarchy prevails. Confucius transmitted not only specific rituals and values, but also a hierarchical social structure and respect for the traditions of the past.

At the heart of Confucianism is the notion of virtue. Good example inspires the pursuit of goodness in others. Moreover, for Confucius, humankind is naturally good. Virtue can be achieved through a gentle process of cultivating the innate tendencies toward the good. The observation of rituals, particularly those honouring one's ancestors, is important for Confucianists. Ironically, it is the ritual itself which assumes prominence, rather than ideas of the afterlife and the gods, though the existence of heaven is assumed. There is little focus upon prayer or communicating with the gods in Confucius' writings, the Analects.

The lifestyle of believers today
Taoists believe that there are three jewels, or virtues, by which all Taoists should live. These jewels are stated in the Tao Te Ching. The three jewels are compassion, moderation and humility. Compassion ultimately leads to courage, moderation leads to generosity, and humility leads to leadership. All these are necessary to return to the Tao. The ultimate goal of Taoism

is to become one with the Tao. For humans, this means leading a natural and simple life. Mental distress and worldly preoccupations are thought to influence and obstruct a person's understanding of the Tao. Being in harmony with the Tao allows the person to return to the original state of all things and become one with the Tao.

To understand the Taoist lifestyle it is important to grasp the distinction between the Tao-min, the religion of the masses, and Tao-shih, the religion of the priests and the adepts. At a popular level the masses rely upon the priests to perform rituals correctly in their name and for their advantage. The performance of rituals is central to the Taoist tradition. Rituals are divided into two categories, *chiao*, offerings or rites of cosmic renewal, and *chai*, rituals that relate more closely to the individual. Examples of the latter category are rituals that rescue an ancestor's soul from hell, rituals for the absolution of sin, and rituals to bless a marriage union or to exorcise evil spirits. Sacred words and prayers to the deities will be included in rituals. The masses will interpret the gods literally, whereas priests and adepts frequently regard the gods as visual expressions of the Tao, which resides in all things. Those serious about religion will practise religious meditation utilising exercises that control breathing and enable one to get in tune mentally and spiritually with the Tao: parallels are often drawn between such practices and Yoga in Hinduism.

As in Taoism there is a focus upon ritual in Confucianism. This is why both traditions are combined in the religious practices of many. Confucianists traditionally regarded it as a sacred duty to honour and respect the emperor for the well-being of the land and the people. Equally, state officials had to perform religious rituals to ensure the blessings of the gods upon the people. The maintenance of proper relations between ruler and subject, father and son, husband and wife, the eldest and his brothers and between elders and friends requires a series of rituals as well as courtesy and reverence. Alongside the practice of rituals Confucius' example of a virtuous life is followed: to love others; to honour one's parents; to do what is right instead of what is of advantage; to practice 'reciprocity,' i.e. 'don't do to others what you would not want yourself'; and to rule by moral example instead of by force and violence.

We have already noted that there are no clear boundaries between Taoism and Confucianism at a popular level. Such common rituals as offering incense to the ancestors, exorcising ghosts and consulting fortune-tellers belong as much to one tradition as another. Some writers have suggested that the best way to appreciate Chinese religion is to focus on those aspects of religious life that are shared by most people, regardless of their affiliation or lack of affiliation with some named tradition.

A typical Chinese funeral and memorial service, could take the following form. Following the death of a family member and the unsuccessful attempt to reclaim his or her spirit, the corpse is prepared for burial. Family members are invited for the first stage of mourning, with higher-ranking families entitled to invite more distant relatives. Rituals of wailing and the wearing of coarse, undyed cloth are practised in the home of the deceased. After some days the coffin is carried in a procession to the grave. Following interment, the attention of the living shifts toward caring for the spirit of the dead. The spirit of the deceased is believed to be spatially fixed and is installed in a rectangular wooden tablet, kept at first in the home and perhaps later in a clan hall. The family continues to come together as a corporate group on behalf of the deceased; they say prayers and provide sustenance, in the form of food and (mock) money.

Another important Chinese ceremony is the New Year's festival, which marks an event not just in the life of the individual and the family, but in the yearly cycle of the cosmos. Those of Chinese origin follow a lunar calendar, which is divided into twelve numbered months of thirty days apiece, divided in half at the full moon (fifteenth night) and new moon (thirtieth night); every so often an additional month is added to synchronise the passage of time in lunar and solar cycles. Families typically begin to celebrate the New Year festival ten or so days before the end of the twelfth month. On the twenty-third day, family members dispatch the God of the Hearth (*Zaojun*), who watches over all that transpires in the home from his throne in the kitchen, to report to the highest god of Heaven, the Jade Emperor (*Yuhuang dadi*). For the last day or two before the end of the year, the doors to the house are sealed and people worship in front of the images of the various gods kept in the house and the ancestor tablets. After a lavish meal, rife with the symbolism of wholeness, longevity, and good fortune, each junior member of the family prostrates himself and herself before the head of the family and his wife. The next day, the first day of the first month, the doors are opened and the family enjoys a vacation of resting and visiting friends. The New Year season concludes on the fifteenth night (the full moon) of the first month, typically marked by a lantern celebration.

A further feature of Chinese religion is the ritual of consulting a spirit medium in the home or in a small temple. Clients request the help of mediums (sometimes called 'shamans') to solve problems like sickness in the family, nightmares, possession by a ghost or errant spirit, or some other misfortune. During the séance the medium usually enters a trance and a spirit or deity speaks through him, sometimes in an altered but comprehensible voice, sometimes in sounds, through movements, or by writing characters in sand that require deciphering by the medium's interpreter. The deity often identifies the problem and prescribes one among a wide range of possible cures. For an illness a particular herbal medicine or offering to a particular spirit may be recommended, while for more serious cases the deity himself, as dramatised in the person of the medium, does battle with the demon and overcomes the difficulty. The entire drama unfolds in front of an audience composed of family members and nearby residents of the community.

Conflict and persecution
With the end of the Ch'ing Dynasty in 1911, state support in China for Taoism ended. Much of the Taoist heritage was destroyed during the next period of war-lordism. After the Communist victory in 1949, religious freedom was severely restricted. The new government put monks to manual labour, confiscated temples, and plundered treasures. Several million monks were reduced to fewer than fifty thousand by 1960. During the cultural revolution in China from 1966 to 1976, much of the remaining Taoist heritage was destroyed. Some religious tolerance was restored under Deng Xiao-ping when he assumed control of the Chinese Communist party in 1982. Since his death the situation is more ambiguous.

The ascendancy of Communism also meant persecution for Confucians as well. Under Chairman Mao Tse-tung, Confucian ways were denounced as reactionary. Maoists accused Confucians of looking backward to feudalism instead of forward to a classless democratic republic. Confucianism was associated with elitism and conservatism. The Red Guards publicly humiliated and ridiculed Confucian teachers. In time, however such radicalism gave way to a more tolerant approach. It became evident to China's Communist leaders, particularly after Mao Tse-tung's death, that Confucian support for the value of the family unit was beneficial to society and the state. Confucian support for the transmission of stability and morality to the next generation were welcome, even if other aspects of traditional Confucianism teaching were not.

Chinese Religion in dialogue
As a dialogue partner with Christianity neither Confucianism nor Taoism has attracted much attention. In some ways Confucianism is regarded as enshrining traditional Chinese

beliefs and practices, that is, the beliefs and practices of a particular culture rather than a religion. Confucianism is a vehicle of Chinese culture and tradition. The fact that Christianity is still suppressed in China and regarded as a foreign religion at the official level has meant that the Christian Churches have not had the opportunity to develop and establish a conversation with Confucians. A further difficulty, which we have already noted, is that popular religion in China and the religious practices of those who regard themselves as of Chinese origin is an amalgam of different traditions that are not always consistent one with another at a theological or theoretical level. The Roman Catholic Church's relations with China have been strained for some time and Pope John Paul II's canonisation of a number of Chinese saints is an attempt to encourage Chinese Christianity. No doubt there is much in Confucianism that is in basic agreement with Catholicism. The importance of honouring one's ancestors strikes a chord with much traditional Catholic piety, where the Church is conceived as embracing both those who are alive and those who are dead. Prayers for the dead in Catholicism provide an interesting parallel with the religious rituals on behalf of one's ancestors in Confucianism, though the underlying theologies differ considerably. Equally the focus on rituals in Confucianism reflects a similar focus in Catholic Christianity.

Christian theology's dialogue with Taoism, although again underdeveloped, has usually focussed on mysticism. The notion of the Tao as implicit in all things is not unlike the teaching of some of the Christian mystics, who profess to see God in all things. Such a connection, however, needs to be explored with caution in that God's transcendence of the world precludes any simple equation of God with the world. Taoism more consistently identifies God with the world, even though the reality of the universe does not exhaust the reality of the Tao. Some theologians have speculated that the same mystical experience is common to a number of religions, but the correct interpretation in terms of orthodox theology is given only in Christianity.

Sikhism

The word 'Sikh' means a disciple. So Sikhism is essentially the path of discipleship. The true Sikh remains unattached to worldly things. The Sikh must do his duty to his family and to the community. The main thing is to lead a pure and moral life, full of noble deeds and kind words. A Sikh does not regard fasting, austerities, pilgrimages, almsgiving and penance as important things.

Adherents and distribution

There are between eighteen and twenty million Sikhs in the world, and 80 per cent of them live in the Punjab in North-West India, where the faith began. There are half a million Sikhs in Britain, 80 per cent of whom are active in their faith. In the UK 39 per cent of Sikhs attend a religious service at a gurdwara (meaning house, or residence of God) once a week. Other countries with large Sikh communities are Canada (225,000) and the USA (100,000). Very small numbers of Sikhs live in Ireland.

The origins, development and teaching of Sikhism

The Sikh faith originated around 1500 CE, in the Punjab area of South Asia, which now falls into the present day states of India and Pakistan, when Guru Nanak began teaching a faith that was quite distinct from Hinduism and Islam. Guru Nanak, began his mission by announcing that God was beyond outward religious distinctions and that what mattered most was for everyone to be a truly devout follower of his or her own faith. He spent the rest of his life teaching, writing hymns, which were often set to music, and travelling as far as Sri Lanka, Baghdad and Mecca to discuss religion with Muslims and Hindus. At his death, Guru Nanak appointed a successor to the community that had grown up around his teaching. Gradually the community grew and gradually it distinguished itself religiously from Hinduism and Islam. Each leader of the community appointed a successor, who continued in the tradition of teaching about the true God and of writing hymns to him. The tenth and last of the human Gurus, Guru Gobind Singh, decided that nobody should become the eleventh Guru, and so he designated the Adi Granth (the sacred scriptures) to be his successor.

Sikhs revere the Adi Granth and believe that it guides them through life in the same way as a human Guru; for this reason it is now called the Guru Granth Sahib. All copies have identical page layouts and identical numbering. The text is in several languages, though the main language used is Punjabi. Almost everything in the book is in poetic form and intended to be sung. The Guru Granth Sahib contains the hymns of different Gurus and writings from people of other faiths, essentially Muslims and Hindus. Despite the great reverence shown to the Guru Granth Sahib by Sikhs, they do not worship it, since only God is worthy of worship.

Sikh spirituality is centred round the need to experience God, and eventually to become one with God. Sikhs believe that God can't be understood properly by human beings, but he can be experienced through love, worship, and contemplation. Liberation is union with God and escape from the cycle of rebirth. The quality of each particular life depends on the law of Karma. Karma is the law of action and effect that determines one's rebirth. The only way out of this cycle is to achieve union with God. Sikhs look both at the created world and into their own hearts to see the divine order that God has given to everything, and through it to understand the nature of God. Most human beings cannot see the true reality of God because they are blinded by their own self-centred pride (Sikhs call it 'haumain') and concern for physical things.

Sikhs believe that God is present in every person, no matter how wicked the person appears, and so everyone is capable of change. To change a person must switch the focus of his or her attention from themselves to God. God dispenses grace to those who seek him through submission to his will, meditating on God's names and following the teachings of the Gurus. Salvation or *Mukti* is a gift from God. In the Sikh Scriptures God is described in various ways: God is loving, righteous and just; God looks after everything in the world; and God is truth.

Everyone is regarded as equal in Sikhism and there is no hierarchical structure or priestly group that performs rituals on behalf of others. Each must follow the path to liberation for himself, relying on God's grace and favour.

The lifestyle of believers today
There are three duties that Sikhs are called to perform and five vices they should avoid. The three duties are: prayer – *Nam Japna*, keeping God in mind at all times; work – *Kirt Karna*, earning an honest living (Sikhs avoid gambling, begging, or working in the alcohol or tobacco industries); and giving to charity and caring for others – *Vand Chhakna*, literally, sharing one's earnings with others. The Five Vices of Lust, Covetousness or Greed, Attachment to things of this world, Anger, and Pride are to be avoided because they obstruct consciousness of God and his grace.

Sikhs are expected to have somewhere at home where the Guru Granth Sahib can be placed and read. Ideally this should be a room set aside, but if there isn't space, the Guru Granth Sahib can be installed in a screened off area of a room that is only used for 'uplifting' purposes. A Sikh aims to get up early, bathe, and then start the day by meditating on God. There are set prayers that a Sikh should recite in the morning and in the evening. Although God is believed to be beyond description, Sikhs feel able to pray to God as a person and a friend who cares for them. Sikhs regard prayer as a way of spending time in company with God. For prayer to be effective the mind must be emptied of all other thoughts but God.

Although Sikhs can worship on their own they see congregational worship as having its own special merits. Congregational Sikh worship takes place in a gurdwara. Sikhs do not have ordained priests, and any Sikh, male or female, can lead the prayers, and recite the scriptures to the congregation. Each Gurdwara has a Granthi who organises the daily services and reads from the Guru Granth Sahib. A Granthi is not a priest but is the reader/custodian of the Adi Granth. He is expected to be an initiated member of the Khalsa who exemplifies the ideals of Sikhism. Gurdwaras are managed by a committee who represent the community. Many Sikhs carry out chores in the gurdwara as their service to the community. These range from working in the kitchen to cleaning the floor. The *langar*, or free food kitchen, is a community act of service. Sikhs also regard caring for the poor or sick as an important religious duty. Some Sikhs belong to a group within Sikhism called the Khalsa. It consists of men and women who have been initiated in the appropriate ceremony. The Khalsa was founded by the tenth and last living guru, Guru Gobind Singh, in 1699 to unite the Sikhs and distinguish them from the followers of other faiths. Membership is for those who are dedicated to their religion. Members are committed to following the Sikh principles laid down in the teachings of the Gurus, wear the physical signs of the Khalsa and the 'five Ks', so that everyone could see that they are Sikhs, and take up arms if necessary to defend the oppressed. Originally, there was also a commitment to reject the Hindu caste system that governed much of Indian life.

The Khalsa are a minority among the Sikhs, but their concept of Sikh ethics and identity has had a decisive influence on the faith as a whole. Members of the Khalsa follow a code of conduct, which amongst other things says that they must not smoke, eat meat unless ritually slaughtered, or commit adultery. They are required to recite and meditate on a series of prayers every morning and night. Khalsa Sikhs display their commitment by wearing five religious symbols, known as the Five Ks:

- *kesh*, or uncut hair, symbolic of the ancient saints;
- *kanga*, the comb, symbolic of cleanliness and faithfulness;
- *kaccha*, a short baggy undergarment, symbolising chastity and agility;
- *kara*, a steel bangle, symbolising obedience to God ;
- *kirpan*, a short sword, symbolic of power and courage.

The turban is not one of the five Ks but is used by Sikh men to cover their uncut hair.

Conflict and persecution

Sikhism is a religion that has been persecuted for much of its history. By the time of Guru Arjan, the fifth Guru or Successor to Guru Nanak, Sikhism was seen as a threat by the state and Guru Arjan was eventually executed for his faith in 1606. The sixth Guru, Hargobind, started to militarise the community so that they would be able to resist oppression. As a result they lived in relative peace until the time of the Moghul Emperor, Aurangzeb, who used force to make his subjects accept Islam. Aurangzeb had the ninth Guru, Tegh Bahadur, arrested and executed in 1675. The tenth Guru, Gobind Singh, instituted the Khalsa in 1699 as a military group within Sikhism to defend the faith. Gobind Singh also established the Sikh rite of initiation and the five Ks, which give Sikhs their unique appearance. Banda Singh Bahadur, a later military leader of the Sikhs led a successful campaign against the Moghuls, until he was captured and executed in 1716. In the middle of the century the Sikhs rose up again, and over the next fifty years took over more and more territory. In 1799 Ranjit Singh captured Lahore, and in 1801 established the Punjab as an independent state, with himself as Maharajah. He proved an adept ruler of a state in which Sikhs were still in a minority. After Ranjit Singh died in 1839 the Sikh state crumbled, damaged by vicious internal battles for the leadership, and in 1845–6 troops of the British

Empire defeated the Sikh armies, and took over much of the Sikh territory. The Sikhs rebelled again in 1849, and were defeated by the British, this time conclusively.

Gradually relations with the British improved as the British came to view the Sikhs as possible allies against both Muslim and Hindu opposition. Good relations, however, came to an end in 1919 with the Amritsar massacre. In April 1919 British troops commanded by General E. H. Dyer opened fire without warning on ten thousand people who were holding a protest meeting. The troops killed about four hundred people and wounded a thousand. Some historians regard the Amritsar Massacre as the event that began the decline of the British Raj, by adding enormous strength to the movement for Indian independence. (In October 1997, Queen Elizabeth II made the gesture of laying a wreath at the site of the massacre.) When British India gained its independence in 1947 it was divided between India and the Islamic state of Pakistan. The Sikhs felt betrayed and reluctantly chose to join India. The Sikhs were unable to demand their own state, because there were too few of them to resist Pakistan's claim to the Punjab. Only by siding with India were they able to keep part of the Punjab, although not before appalling loss of life in communal massacres. Sikhs lost many of their privileges, much of their land, and were deeply alienated.

The Sikh ambition for a state of their own was something that India was not prepared to concede, though in 1966, after years of Sikh demands, India divided the Punjab into three, recreating Punjab as a state with a Sikh majority. This was not enough to stop Sikh anger at what they saw as continuing oppression and the unfair way in which they thought India had set the boundaries of the new state. They continued to demand various concessions from the Indian government. As Sikh discontent grew, the conflict gradually changed from a purely political conflict into a confrontation between Hindus and Sikhs; and then to real violence.

A Sikh preacher called Jarnail Singh Bhindranwale became the leader of a group of the most disaffected of the Sikhs. In 1983 Bhindranwale and his closest followers took refuge in the Golden Temple Complex at Amritsar, the most revered place in the Sikh world. The Indian government believed that the Temple was being used as a militant command post, a sanctuary for wanted criminals and as a warehouse for weapons, and resolved to take action. In June 1984 Indian troops launched 'Operation Bluestar'. They attacked the Golden Temple complex, killing many of those inside, and seriously damaging the buildings. This invasion of the holiest place of the Sikhs infuriated many Sikhs, even the non-militant. They saw the Indian Prime Minister, Indira Gandhi, who had ordered the invasion, as a deliberate persecutor of the Sikh faith and community. In October 1984, Indira Gandhi was assassinated by two of her Sikh bodyguards. Four days of anti-Sikh rioting followed in India. The government said that more than two thousand seven hundred people, mostly Sikhs, were killed, while newspapers and human-rights groups put the death toll between ten and seventeen thousand. Sikhs are still resentful that action has not been taken against those who were responsible. For several years militant Sikhs responded by killing members of the Hindu community and a number of Sikh political leaders who opposed them. Anger and frustration dominated Sikh politics until the mid-1990s.

The Punjab is currently reasonably peaceful, although in the last two or three years the rise of Hindu nationalism has alarmed some Sikhs who fear further persecution.

Sikh religion in dialogue
Sikh temples are open to all who respect God. Sikhism has not been a missionary religion, believing that each should follow the religious path of his upbringing and culture. God is found in all religions, though naturally Sikhs believe that Sikhism has most fully understood the nature of the divine and the means

of achieving liberation. Guru Nanak shared beliefs with Hindus and Muslims and he worshipped at the shrines of both traditions. He sought to overcome the differences between Hinduism and Islam and to bring people from both communities together. For him, the true meeting place of religion is in experience of the divine. He felt himself at one in the company of Muslim sufis and Hindu yogis. Mystical experience, he believed, is at the heart of all genuine spirituality. The respectful attitude to other religions exhibited by Sikhs has not been reciprocated and the history of Sikhism has been punctuated by Hindu and Muslim persecution. Such a history naturally stifles dialogue. Ironically one of the greatest obstacles to dialogue with Sikhism is that both Hinduism and Islam have in the past been intent on interpreting Sikh beliefs and practices as a heretical form of one or other of the two traditions. In a sense this contradicts one of the fundamental rules of dialogue, which is that dialogue partners should be allowed to define themselves. Sikhism should not have to conform its identity to Hindu or Muslim expectations, but must be allowed to affirm its own distinctive identity over against Hinduism and Islam. There is no real dialogue when one of the partners has to relinquish his distinctiveness in order to be heard and appreciated. Dialogue is a meeting of equals in a genuine search for understanding.

African Traditional Religion

In a straightforward sense the title African Traditional Religion is a misnomer if by this is meant that there is a single African religion with common beliefs and practices, to be distinguished from the other world religions. Rather, the designation African Traditional Religion covers the religious beliefs and practices of a number of different groups and tribes. Each group has a different pantheon of gods and spirits to whom prayer and sacrifice are made and most of the groups are bounded geographically and regionally. Although certain common elements can be identified between the practices of different African Traditional Religions, it is difficult to group them as one.

Adherents and distribution
The number of followers of African Traditional Religions is widely disputed. This is because tribal religion is often practised alongside another religion, say Islam or Catholic Christianity. There is also evidence to suggest that in times of suffering and stress individuals turn to tribal religions for comfort and aid, chiefly using spells and sacrifices to placate or win favour from the gods. Most authorities cite twenty-five to thirty million as the number of those who practise Traditional Religion. Countries where Traditional Religion adherents comprises between one third and a half of the population of the country are Benin, Botswana, Guinea-Bisau, Ivory Coast, Liberia, Madagascar, Mozambique, and Sierra Leone.

The origins, development and teaching of African Traditional Religion
African religion has no sacred books. It is found primarily in oral sources, including stories, myths, proverbs, prayers, ritual incantations and songs. Other sources are art, language, ceremonies and rituals, religious objects and places like shrines, altars, and ceremonial symbols, and magical objects. The authority of African Religion is the authority of tradition and practice. Religion is lived (not read), it is experienced (not meditated), it is integrated into the life of the people.

While there are local variations, we can identify common elements that define African Traditional Religion; it is upon these we will concentrate.

The most prominent feature of African Traditional Religions is that the world is a sacred place containing God, divinities and spirits, even nature is alive with spiritual power. The power of the Holy is manifest everywhere and potentially in everything. Although it is a religious universe, with its beginning in and through God, the realm of religion and spirituality are rarely focused upon the Creator God. He is transcendent and typically removed from the world of human affairs. Some of the names given to him suggest his remoteness: the Massai (Kenya and Tanzania) refer to God as *Engai*, 'the Unseen One, the Unknown One', among the Tenda (Guinea), God is called *Hounounga* which means 'the Unknown'.

In general, people consider the universe to be in two interlocking parts: the visible and the invisible. Human beings live on the visible level, while God and spiritual beings exist on the invisible level. There is a link between the two worlds. God and spiritual beings make their presence felt on the physical level; and persons project themselves into the spiritual level. African religiosity is very sensitive to the spiritual dimension of life. Divinities and spirits inhabit the sacred space between human beings and God. Most divinities were created by God, though some are also personifications of natural phenomena and objects such as mountains, lakes, rivers, earthquakes, or thunder. The spirits are lesser powers. Some writers distinguish between heavenly (sky) spirits and earthly spirits. The heavenly spirits are those associated with 'heavenly' phenomena and objects like the sun, the stars, comets, rain and storms. The earthly ones are those associated with earthly phenomena and objects, and those that are spirits of the dead.

African religiosity places persons at the centre of creation. According to many accounts and myths, God created persons after creating other things. In the beginning, persons (male and female) were like children, with God as their parent in a family setting. They lived in a form of paradise, leading a state of life without suffering, fear, sickness or even death. God was close to them and communicated with them. God's dwelling place, heaven (the sky), and the earth (ground), the dwelling place of persons, were joined. However, things did not remain at the level of paradise forever. Stories tell of the gifts of life and immortality being lost by humans: in some stories the gifts are stolen by another creature, in other stories humankind failed to follow God's instructions. In any case, heaven and earth were severed from each other and God withdrew his presence. Paradise was lost, with the result that suffering, sickness and death came into the world and have remained ever since. God, however, did not abandon the human race entirely. He continues to provide food, children, rain, sunshine, and medicines to heal the sick, only now from a distance. Children perpetuate life and thus counteract death. People may sacrifice and make offerings to God and speak to God personally or communally through prayer, invocation, ritual, dance or singing. God communicates through dreams, visions and nature.

There is a deeply rooted belief in a mystical power or force in the universe that derives from God. People use this power in divination, exorcism, protecting persons and property, predicting where to find lost articles, and foretelling the outcome of an undertaking. It is also this power that they employ in the practice of magic, sorcery, and witchcraft. Individuals such as diviners, traditional doctors and witches know better than other people how to contact the spirits. The line between the natural and the supernatural is difficult to draw in African religion. What we in the West might attribute to nature may be interpreted in Africa as the act of a deity; illness may be connected to an evil spirit, and so on. The practice of magic causes much fear in African life: spells may be cast and forces unleashed to achieve one's goals, some of which may be malicious. Nevertheless, the positive use of mystical and magical powers is cherished and plays a major role in regulating ethical relations in the community and in supplying answers to questions about the causes of good luck and misfortune. In fear of witchcraft, people may refrain from stealing, speaking rudely and showing disrespect where respect is due.

Medicine women and men are found in every village. They undergo long training and apprenticeship. They learn to diagnose illnesses and complaints that affect not only human beings, but also animals and nature. They acquire knowledge of herbs, roots, fruits, shells, insects and juices, and their medicinal properties. They use divination to communicate with the invisible world at the psychic level of consciousness. Healing rituals and invocations are directed not only against disease or misfortune, but against the 'powers' of witchcraft and curses. Often there will be community participation in rituals, where the benefits to be gained extend to the whole community. A bad harvest or drought requires community action.

Sacred places and sacred objects play an important role in African religion. Places set apart as sacred include mountains, caves, waterfalls, rocks, groves, trees, rainmaking stones, and certain animals. Sacred objects include altars, sacrificial pots, masks and drums. To put such objects to profane use would invite judgement or sickness. Communities observe and treat some places as sanctuaries in which no human beings or animals may be killed, and where no trees may be felled. Sacrifices, offerings, prayers and rituals are performed here. Some homesteads have family altars or graves that serve as sacred places where family members make prayers, offerings, and small sacrifices.

The person consists of body and spirit. Death destroys the body, but the spirit continues in the next life. Most people observe rituals related to the disposal of the dead. The body is usually buried in the compound of the surviving relatives. In some societies the body is formally left to rot in the woods. In some traditions it is the custom to bury belongings, weapons, tools and foodstuffs with the dead body. People take for granted the continuation of life after physical death. The relation between the living and the departed is cultivated in different ways, being stronger in some societies than others. These may include appearances of the departed in visions or dreams to the living, naming of children after the departed if they resemble them. People may call upon the departed or mention them in making formal covenants or oaths. In some prayers people ask the living dead to assist them by conveying their prayers, sacrifices and offerings to God, since people consider them to be closer to God than those who are alive on earth.

The lifestyle of believers today

Ritual is an indispensable dimension of African Traditional Religion. Rites and rituals provide the context through which humans experience the presence of the Sacred and secure chosen ends. Rites are performed to heal the sick, restore social and family harmony, and to secure good fortune. Rainmakers perform rituals to bring rain, diviners to know the future and modify a client's fate, and healers to cure. The movement of the seasons are recorded in rituals and hunters perform rituals to secure or to celebrate a kill. Sacrifices may be offered to divinities or to the spirits. Offerings are made of such items as cereal, beer, milk, and fruit. The more momentous or serious the situation the more likely it will be that a blood sacrifice will be required. The Nuer of Ethiopia and Sudan require the sacrifice of domestic animals for crises such as severe sickness, female barrenness, war, and the translation of souls from this world to the next.

Many African societies have religious rituals for each phase of life and rites of passage are an essential feature of African Traditional Religion. Rites celebrate birth, the transition from adolescence to adulthood, marriage and death. The transition to adulthood is particularly significant. Some tribes require young men to withdraw from village life for a time and many require acts of bravery in hunting to be displayed. Sacrifices may be made to the gods to ensure success and good fortune. Major events in life often involve consultation of fortune-tellers and diviners to ascertain the will of God and the spirits.

Many Traditional African religions encourage morning prayers in which God is thanked for the gift of another day and his help is invoked for the day's tasks. Impromptu prayers may also be said throughout the days both to praise God and to make personal and community needs known to God.

Conflict and persecution

The history of Western colonialism in Africa was a history of persecution for adherents of African Traditional Religions (Muslim invaders in earlier centuries acted similarly). In some ways it is only after World War Two and the end of colonialism that persecution has ended. Followers of African Traditional Religion were labelled by Christian missionaries as polytheists, idolaters, and practitioners of witchcraft. Where the colonial powers had the military might and the local administration had the motivation African Traditional Religion was suppressed. In some places persecution was not pursued, sometimes on the assumption that African people knew no better and should be left to their own mistaken spiritual devices and sometimes on the assumption that African Traditional Religion would simply disappear before Christian evangelism. Indeed throughout the twentieth century many adherents of African Traditional Religion have espoused Christianity, sometimes producing a curious amalgam of the two traditions. Generally the Protestant Churches have taken a much firmer line than the Catholic Church against the teachings of traditional religious beliefs and practices: though neither Church in recent decades can be accused of lending support to persecution. In fact the persecution of followers of African Traditional Religion in the years of colonialism was probably more political than religious, in that some of those who opposed colonial rule sought to align Traditional Religion with nationalism.

African Traditional Religion in dialogue

There has been a long history of Christian encounter with and reflection upon African Traditional Religion. The earliest nineteenth-century Christian missionaries to Africa typically dismissed the adherents of Traditional Religions as pagans, animists, pantheists, superstitious people, magicians, even devil-worshippers. The desire of the missionaries was to save African people from the 'darkness of superstition' and to instruct them in the true faith of Christ. Alongside missionary activity the missionaries introduced a Western system of education and the practice of modern medicine. Although converts were made there was a sense in which the Church in Africa up to the mid-twentieth century was not the African Church: many of the clergy and almost all of the bishops remained European. Local customs were disdained and uniformity achieved. This situation was to change in the wake of Vatican II and the Council's desire to build bridges between the Gospel and the culture of those whom it wanted to evangelise.

The very first magisterial document to mention the religious traditions of African peoples, and in a positive light for that matter, is *Africae Terrarum* of Pope Paul VI, issued on October 29, 1967. In this document Paul VI, reflecting the spirit of the Vatican Council, spoke of how 'many customs and rites, once considered to be strange are seen today, in the light of ethnological science, as integral parts of various social systems, worthy of study and commanding respect. In this regard, we think it profitable to dwell on some general ideas which typify ancient African religious cultures because we think their moral and religious values are deserving of attentive consideration.' There has been an increasing recognition by Christians of positive elements within African traditional religious practice. Such values as family, community, appreciation of life as a gift from God, and the sense of the Sacred, are deeply respected in African Traditional Religions. As a consequence of Pope Paul VI's initiative the Church throughout the eighties and nineties sought to adapt some of these values and re-interpret them in Christian categories. Traditional rituals were integrated into

Christian religious practice and African beliefs about God were regarded as witnesses to the type of God made known in Christ.

There are a number of fruitful avenues for dialogue with African Tribal Religions. One important aspect of African religion is respect for nature and an appreciation that nature is related to God. In African Traditional religions all of life is viewed religiously. God is regarded as active in the world and in the affairs of men and women. Interestingly, this conviction coupled with the existence of spirits suggests parallels between African Tribal Religions and the world of the New Testament (and of course Charismatic Christianity). The Apostle Paul spoke of 'Lords many and gods many' in the Graeco-Roman world. A sense of kinship has always been prominent in African Traditional Religions and such a sense seems to echo something of the meaning of the Christian notion of the Church as the community of the living and the dead in Christ. Our comments on dialogue with African Tribal Religions has focused on the situation as perceived by the Christian partner in dialogue, rather than the situation as perceived by a follower of African Traditional Religion. There is a sense in which the Church, however much it respects aspects of African Traditional religion, still maintains that the fullness of revelation is found in Christ. This does not mean that dialogue is a covert form of evangelism, rather it means that once both partners in the dialogue gain a proper understanding of each other, of similarities and differences, decisions have to be made about truth and commitment. All of us have to decide which God to serve and which spiritual path to follow.